Grammar Practice Activities

Second Edition

Cambridge Handbooks for Language Teachers

This series, now with over 40 titles, offers practical ideas, techniques and activities for the teaching of English and other languages providing inspiration for both teachers and trainers.

Recent titles in this series:

Learner Autonomy
A guide to developing learner responsibility
ÁGOTA SCHARLE *and* ANITA SZABÓ

Personalizing Language Learning
GRIFF GRIFFITHS *and* KATHRYN KEOHANE

Teaching Adult Second Language Learners
HEATHER MCKAY *and* ABIGAIL TOM

Teach Business English
SYLVIE DONNA

Teaching English Spelling
A practical guide
RUTH SHEMESH *and* SHEILA WALLER

Using Folktales
ERIC K. TAYLOR

Learner English (Second Edition)
A teacher's guide to interference and other problems
edited by MICHAEL SWAN *and* BERNARD SMITH

Planning Lessons and Courses
Designing sequences of work for the language classroom
TESSA WOODWARD

Teaching Large Multilevel Classes
NATALIE HESS

Using the Board in the Language Classroom
JEANNINE DOBBS

Writing Simple Poems
Pattern Poetry for Language Acquisition
VICKI L. HOLMES *and* MARGARET R. MOULTON

Laughing Matters
Humour in the language classroom
PÉTER MEDGYES

Stories
Narrative activities in the language classroom
RUTH WAJNRYB

Using Authentic Video in the Language Classroom
JANE SHERMAN

Extensive Reading Activities for Teaching Language
edited by JULIAN BAMFORD *and* RICHARD R. DAY

Language Activities for Teenagers
edited by SETH LINDSTROMBERG

Pronunciation Practice Activities
A resource book for teaching English pronunciation
MARTIN HEWINGS

Drama Techniques (Third Edition)
A resource book of communication activities for language teachers
ALAN MALEY *and* ALAN DUFF

Five-Minute Activities for Business English
PAUL EMMERSON *and* NICK HAMILTON

Games for Language Learning (Third Edition)
ANDREW WRIGHT, DAVID BETTERIDGE *and* MICHAEL BUCKBY

Dictionary Activities
CINDY LEANEY

Dialogue Activities
Exploring spoken interaction in the language class
NICK BILBROUGH

Five-Minute Activities for Young Learners
PENNY MCKAY *and* JENNI GUSE

The Internet and the Language Classroom (Second Edition)
A practical guide for teachers
GAVIN DUDENEY

Working with Images
A resource book for the language classroom
BEN GOLDSTEIN

Grammar Practice Activities

SECOND EDITION

A practical guide for teachers

Penny Ur

Consultant and editor: Michael Swan

CAMBRIDGE
UNIVERSITY PRESS

CAMBRIDGE
UNIVERSITY PRESS

University Printing House, Cambridge CB2 8BS, United Kingdom

One Liberty Plaza, 20th Floor, New York, NY 10006, USA

477 Williamstown Road, Port Melbourne, VIC 3207, Australia

314–321, 3rd Floor, Plot 3, Splendor Forum, Jasola District Centre, New Delhi – 110025, India

79 Anson Road, #06–04/06, Singapore 079906

Cambridge University Press is part of the University of Cambridge.

It furthers the University's mission by disseminating knowledge in the pursuit of education, learning and research at the highest international levels of excellence.

www.cambridge.org
Information on this title: www.cambridge.org/9780521732321

First published 2009
Reprinted 2018

Printed in Italy by Rotolito S.p.A.

A catalogue record for this publication is available from the British Library

Library of Congress Cataloguing in Publication data

Ur, Penny.
Grammar practice activities : a practical guide for teachers / Penny Ur ; consultant and editor: Michael Swan. – 2nd ed.
p. cm. – (Cambridge handbooks for language teachers)
Includes index.
ISBN 978-0-521-73232-1 (pbk. with cd-rom)
1. English language–Study and teaching–Foreign speakers. 2. English language–Grammar–Problems, exercises, etc. I. Swan, Michael. II. Title. III. Series.
PE1128.A2U73 2009
428.007–dc22
2008053631

ISBN 978-0-521-73232-1 Paperback and CD-ROM

Contents

Thanks and acknowledgements

Heartfelt thanks to Michael Swan for punctilious editing and lots of good ideas.

1.1.4 *Adjective poem* and 16.7 *Preposition poem* are based on the ideas of Vicki L. Holmes and Margaret R. Moulton, *Writing Simple Poems: Pattern Poetry for Language Acquisition*, (2001), Cambridge: Cambridge University Press 2001 reproduced with permission.

1.2.5 *Preferences* is an activity I learnt from Mario Rinvolucri.

7.2.4 *Paired Cloze* makes use of material from *Practice Your Unseens 3* by Jack Baum and Michael Toben. © 1994 Eric Cohen Books Ltd.

Finally, my particular gratitude to my in-house editors, Claire Cole and Alyson Maskell for their punctilious editing, professional approach and unending patience. They suggested substantial improvements and eliminated a large number of slips and inconsistencies. Any remaining mistakes are my own responsibility.

Introduction

I decided to write the first edition of this book because I needed it; and as soon as I began to discuss the idea with other teachers, it became clear that many of them felt the same need as I did, and for similar reasons. We all felt that grammar practice was essentially a useful thing to do, but we were dissatisfied with the kinds of exercises we found in our textbooks: mainly conventional form-focused gapfills, sentence completions and matching.

'What we need,' a group of teachers told me, 'is a book that will gather together the most useful of the game-like or communicative grammar-practice procedures that are in the books we know, plus any more you can think of or find, laid out systematically so that we can look up, say, 'Present perfect' on Monday morning and find a few good ideas to choose from.'

So that was what I did.

The response was warm and gratifying: the book became one of the best-selling titles in the Cambridge Handbooks for Language Teachers series, and is still selling well today. It is without doubt my own favourite of the books I have written.

This second edition differs from the first in the following ways:

- *Part 1* (general guidelines) is rather shorter and *Part 2* (the activities themselves) longer.
- A number of activities have been added and a few of the less successful ones in the original edition deleted.
- Subject matter has been updated, as have the illustrations.
- Brief headings have been added to the beginning of each activity to indicate its main teaching point, the age and level for which it is intended, and any necessary materials or preparations.
- Useful tips on language or teaching strategies have been added.
- A CD-ROM accompanies the book, providing PDFs of all the photocopiable material in colour from the book and the artwork. The symbol ◎ indicates that the material which follows it can be found on the CD-ROM.

Part 1 of the book is divided into three sections, corresponding to the three words in the title of the book. *Grammar* provides a brief general introduction to the teaching of grammar; *Practice* explains the basic principles of effective practice in language teaching in general and grammar teaching in particular; *Activities* lists the main features of the activities in this book, and some practical hints to help you (the teacher) do them successfully in class.

Part 2 consists of the grammar-practice activities themselves, designed according to the principles outlined in *Part 1*. The activities are grouped into sections according to grammatical category, and these are ordered alphabetically; so you should be able to find any section you want simply by leafing through the book. If, however, you use different terminology from mine, you will probably find your term in the index at the end of the book. Names of specific activities (Questionnaires, Association dominoes, etc.) are also included in the index, in bold print. Where activities are mentioned elsewhere in the text, they are referred to by their section number and name, not by page number (*7.1.3 Questionnaires*, *11.3.1 Association dominoes*, etc.).

PART 1 Background theory and guidelines

1 Grammar

What is grammar?

Grammar may be roughly defined as the way a language manipulates and combines words (or bits of words) so as to express certain kinds of meaning, some of which cannot be conveyed adequately by vocabulary alone. These include the way ideas are grouped and related, and the purposes of utterances (statement, question, request, etc.). Grammar may also serve to express time relations, singular/plural distinctions and many other aspects of meaning. There are rules which govern how words have to be manipulated and organized so as to express these meanings: a competent speaker of the language will be able to apply these rules so as to convey his or her chosen meanings effectively and acceptably.

The grammar practised in this book

The grammar on which this book is based is that which is described in most modern grammar books (see *References and further reading*), p. 317 and which is likely to be known and accepted by most readers. As far as possible, I have tried to avoid language features which are specifically associated with one English variety (British, American, Australian, Indian, etc.), but rather use those forms which are likely to be used internationally by both native and non-native speakers.

Nobody (including native speakers) always uses perfectly correct grammar: the teaching aim of this book is, therefore, not to achieve perfection, but to assist learners to master the most important grammatical usages that will enable them to convey meanings effectively and acceptably. From the point of view of sheer length, moreover, it has not been possible to provide a comprehensive coverage of English grammatical structures; the activities focus only on the main items needed for written and spoken communication, and I apologize in advance if you find some points missing that you would have liked to have been included.

The place of grammar in language teaching

There is no doubt that some kind of implicit knowledge of grammar is necessary for the mastery of a language at anything beyond a very basic level: you cannot use words effectively unless you know how they should be put together in acceptable sentence or phrase structures. This does not necessarily mean that you have to be able to articulate the rules: native speakers of any language express themselves in their own language (L1) correctly, but can rarely explain what the rules are that govern such expression.

But people learning the grammar of an additional language through a formal course of study probably do not do so the same way as they learnt their first language. There has been some discussion in recent years of how such learning can be most effectively brought about. Some questions discussed in the literature have been:

- Can grammar be acquired only through exposure to plenty of comprehensible input (listening/reading)? Can it be learnt only through communicative activities involving all four skills (listening/reading/writing/speaking)?
- Should grammar be taught only 'reactively' (in response to errors or learner uncertainty), or should it be taught 'proactively', based on a grammatical syllabus?
- Do learners need to learn grammar rules explicitly – that is, understand and be able to explain why certain forms are correct and others not?
- Are focused grammar practice exercises necessary?

This is not the place to explore in depth the pros and cons of possible answers to these different questions. The approach which forms the basis for this book, based on my interpretation of the research literature and professional experience, is summarized by the bulleted points below. Note, however, that these points are generalizations which may not hold true for all learners in all learning situations: like many practical principles in education they are useful as bases for planning our teaching as long as we remember that there may be exceptions.

I believe, then, that in most situations ...

- ... it is helpful to teach grammar systematically, based on a grammatical syllabus;

- ... it is helpful to have an explicit rule available for a grammar point being learnt, provided this is simple enough to be grasped by the learner;
- ... learners will benefit from focused practice applying this rule in grammar exercises and activities[1];
- ... 'mechanical' exercises such as gap fill and sentence completion are useful in learning grammar;
- ... more important, however, are activities which provide opportunities for learners to create or understand meanings using the target grammar point;
- ... learning of grammar is enhanced further by occasional 'reactive' teaching of grammatical forms during communicative activities (correction of mistakes, for example, or 'noticing' by teacher or learner of an interesting form used in a text or activity).

Grammar may furnish the basis for a set of classroom procedures during which it becomes temporarily the main learning objective. But the key word here is 'temporarily'. The learning of grammar should be seen in the long term as one of the **means** of acquiring a thorough mastery of the language as a whole, not as an end in itself. Thus, although there may be times at which we ask our students to learn a certain structure through exercises that concentrate on virtually meaningless manipulations of language, we should in principle invest more time and energy in activities that use it meaningfully, culminating in generally communicative tasks where the emphasis is on successful communication, and any learning of grammar takes place only as incidental to this main objective.

Note that although I have for convenience presented this model of grammar teaching as if it were a chronological sequence (first learning the rule, then mechanical practice, then meaningful practice, then communication) – it doesn't necessarily work like that in the classroom. We may well, for example, discover in the course of a communicative activity that some learners have a problem with a specific grammatical point, and at that point decide to take some time out to practise it. Or we may do some grammatical activities and elicit the rule as a result rather than as a preliminary. There are lots of ways of sequencing, though perhaps the traditional sequence implied above is still the most common.

The bottom line here is that I strongly believe in the value of practice as a component of grammar teaching in the teaching of English as an international language in formal courses of study.

[1] The distinction between 'exercise' and 'activity' is dealt with in *Activities*, p. 11.

2 Practice

Practice may be defined as any kind of engagement with the language on the part of the learner, usually under teacher supervision, whose primary objective is to consolidate learning. During practice the material is absorbed into long-term memory and the learner enabled to understand and produce it with gradually lessening teacher support. A practice procedure may involve reception (exposure to comprehensible spoken or written input) or production (speaking or writing).

Although it is over-optimistic to claim that 'practice makes perfect', effective practice is likely to make a substantial contribution towards mastery of grammatical forms.

But what makes practice effective? There is, of course, no one generalization that will answer this question, but some of the key features that contribute to successful practice are the following.

Validity

By *validity* I mean that the procedure should in fact practise what it says it practises, and not something else. Supposing our aim is to practise the present perfect, and an item runs as follows:

> Two years ago we left the country and came to live in the city. We are still living in the city today. So we ________________ in the city for two years.

Either *have lived* or *have been living* would be acceptable here: but the point is that in order to fill in the missing verb, the learner has to read and understand two lines of text, with another two verb forms in them, and the time and thought which are actually invested in the target item itself is relatively small. The validity, therefore, of the practice provided by such exercise items is low. For examples of more valid practice procedures focusing on the same teaching point, see *14.3.2 What has happened?* and *14.3.3 Oh!*, where pictures or one-word cues give rise to a large number of responses using the target structure.

You may say: why does this matter? Surely reading and understanding the surrounding text is also useful? Yes: but the point is that if a lot of time is spent on reading and understanding surrounding text – or on puzzling out problems, or translating, or discussing, or any other activity that does not directly practise the target item – then the *quantity* of target-item practice is correspondingly low.

Quantity

The aim of a practice activity is to provide opportunities to engage with the target structure: if the number of times the learner does in fact have such opportunities is small, then the practice is correspondingly less effective in achieving its main aim.

Even if it is valid, a brief activity that provides very little such quantity of practice will not give learners much opportunity to consolidate their learning. The function of such low-quantity exercises is likely to be mainly in providing the teacher with information about how well the learners have mastered the target item, but not in actually consolidating learning. In other words, the procedure will probably function as an informal test rather than as practice.

Success-orientation

Another important feature of effective practice is that learners' responses should be right, rather than that they should be wrong and needing to be corrected. So the activity should be designed to elicit acceptable and successful responses.

This is not to say that there is no place for mistakes and error correction. But using correct grammar in speech is like any other skill: it involves the swift and effortless production of acceptable and appropriate performance that can be achieved only if the skill has been 'automatized' to such an extent that the learner can perform it without thinking. Such 'automatization' is achieved largely through practice. Thus practice essentially means performing the target behaviour (in this case, using the grammatical feature) successfully again and again: at first, with some thought and application of conscious memorized instructions, but later more and more swiftly and smoothly until the original instruction or rule, as a conscious articulated statement, may even be forgotten. Doing something wrong and being corrected will help raise awareness of what is correct; but it will not help automatization of the skill. Or to put it another way: correcting a learner 50 times may help him or her become more aware of a problem, but it will not improve actual performance. It is only when the learner starts getting it right on his or her own, and does so repeatedly, that he or she is on the way to real mastery.

Teachers may provide for success-orientation by various means:

- by designing or selecting the activity so that it is reasonably easy: it elicits responses that you know the learners can deal with successfully;
- by providing for pre-learning: review the target grammar point before doing the activity, so that the material is fresh in learners' memories;
- by helping the learners get it right as they are doing it: simply give extra wait-time before requiring responses, for example, or give a hint or some sort of supportive 'scaffolding'.

Besides immediate effectiveness in consolidating learning, the principle of success-orientation has significant general pedagogical implications. A student whose performance is consistently successful will develop a positive self-image as a language learner, whereas one who frequently fails may be discouraged and demotivated. It should also be noted that tension and anxiety are fairly high if learners feel there is a possibility of 'failure' (that is, if they are in a sense being tested), and are correspondingly lowered if they are confident of success. Thus, success-orientation contributes significantly to a positive classroom climate of relaxation, confidence and motivation.

On the other hand, the fact that there is no risk of failure in producing acceptable language lessens the challenge of the activity for some participants, so we have to find other ways of making it interesting (see *Interest*, pp. 9–10).

Heterogeneity

A *heterogeneous* exercise, as I am using the term here, is one which may be done at various different levels. Because all classes are more or less heterogeneous, a *homogeneous* exercise cannot possibly provide effective practice for all the students: it will be too difficult for the weaker ones, and/or lacking in quantity and challenge for the stronger. It is, however, possible – and desirable – to design practice tasks that can be interpreted and performed at different levels, so that some students will be able to do more than others in terms of both quality and quantity.

An example of a homogeneous exercise is one based on multiple-choice questions; for example:

1) Jenny is a baby, so she _______ go to school.

a doesn't	c don't
b isn't	d aren't

Such an item can only be done by students above a certain level of proficiency: a learner who has not mastered the rules about when you use *do* or *is* with negative verbs in the present will probably get it wrong, or may not even do it at all. On the other hand, a learner who is well on the way to mastering the rule and can use it to create all sorts of meaningful statements has no opportunity to do so, but is limited to the rather boring sentence provided and cannot practise at a level appropriate to him/her.

But supposing we say:

2) Jenny is a baby, so she doesn't go to school. What else doesn't she do?

... we have thus not only provided for pre-learning and success-orientation by supplying a model of the kind of sentence we are looking for, we are also opening possibilities for the learners to respond with sentences at all sorts of levels. One might say at a simple level: 'Jenny doesn't read books', while another might use more advanced language: 'Jenny doesn't use a credit card'.

To put it another way: heterogeneous items like 2) above are typically *open-ended*: they are intended to elicit a wide range of different, equally acceptable, responses. *Closed-ended* ones, on the other hand, like 1) above, which have only one right answer, are inherently homogeneous: they provide appropriate practice for only a limited number of the members of the class.

The use of heterogeneous, open-ended exercises, incidentally, not only ensures that a higher proportion of the class get learning value out of the practice; it also, like success-orientation, has a positive effect on learner attitude and motivation. Responses at many different levels can be 'right', hence these exercises provide an opportunity for the teacher to give slower or less confident students the approval and encouragement they need. They are also likely to be more interesting.

Interest

An otherwise well-designed practice procedure may fail to produce successful learning simply because it is boring: interest is an essential feature of successful practice, not just an optional improvement. Learners who are bored find it difficult to concentrate, their attention wanders, and they may spend much of the lesson time thinking of things other than the learning task in hand; even if they are apparently engaged with the exercise, the quality of the effort and attention given to learning drops appreciably. Moreover, because boredom, particularly in younger classes, often produces unruly behaviour, more valuable learning time may be wasted on coping with discipline problems. If, however, the class is interested in what it is doing, its members will not only learn more efficiently, they are also likely to enjoy the process and to want to continue.

For some practical ideas on increasing the interest of classroom activities, see pp. 13–19 in the next chapter.

Summary

Effective practice procedures, then, are usually characterized by the features of *validity, quantity, success-orientation, heterogeneity* and *interest*. Any one particular exercise may of course display one or more of these features to a lesser degree and still be effective in gaining specific objectives: but if too many of them are absent, the activity may provide very little learning value.

Let us take, for example, an exercise which consists of five sentences with either *have* or *has* missing, and which requires individual students to fill in the missing item.

There is in such an exercise relatively little quantity of practice and no particular success-orientation; the exercise is homogeneous and lacking in interest. You may, by doing such an exercise with a class, find out which of its members know the difference between *have* and *has* (hence it might function quite well as an assessment procedure), but you will have done little to help those whose knowledge is still a little shaky and who simply need practice. In contrast, you might first tell the students about some interesting or unusual possessions of your own ('I *have* ...'), then invite them to describe some of their own to each other, and finally challenge them to remember what possessions another student *has*. This activity is obviously more interesting and more heterogeneous; it is also likely to be success-oriented and valid, as well as providing for quantity of practice (see *17.1.2 Possessions*).

Unfortunately, exercises like the gapfill described above are extremely common in the classroom and grammar textbooks – probably because they are easy to design and administer – and teachers and textbook authors are often unaware that they are testing more than teaching.

So far we have looked at topics connected with the place of grammar in language teaching, and how it may, or should, be taught; and we have considered some aspects of grammar practice. It now remains to turn to the third word in the title of this book and see how some of the theoretical ideas dealt with up to now can be applied in the design and presentation of classroom activities.

3 Activities

Practice procedures are usually called *exercises* or *activities*. The term *exercise* normally refers to the conventional textbook procedure involving a numbered list of items which the learner has to respond to correctly: by answering questions, for example, by matching corresponding items or by filling gaps. These focus very much on correct forms, and the meaning is secondary: sometimes such exercises may be done correctly without any understanding of meaning at all. *Activity* on the other hand, as the word is used in this book, refers to a procedure where the learner is activated in some kind of task that induces him or her to engage with the target language items in a meaningful way. Activities may also be based on lists of items, or they may not, but the responses are typically open-ended (no one right answer) and often personalized. The distinction between the two is one of general orientation rather than a mutually exclusive dichotomy, and some procedures may be classified as either. As I have indicated previously, there is room for both in the teaching of grammar.

The main section of this chapter consists of descriptions of some characteristic features of the activities in this book. In a shorter following section I shall provide some practical tips about how to use them in the classroom.

Features of activity design

The task

A task is anything the learners are asked to do that produces a clear outcome. In principle, a task may be overtly language-based ('Give me some examples of "yes/no" questions'); but I am using it here to refer to activity that is essentially concerned with making or receiving meanings: so 'yes/no' questions, for example, would be produced in a task in order to find out or guess something, rather than just as samples of language forms (see, for example, *7.1.1 Guessing*). The function of the task is simply to activate the learners in such a way as to get them to engage with the material to be practised in an interesting and challenging way.

Note that the word 'activate' or the phrase 'active language use' usually implies the actual production of instances of the structure on the part of the learners themselves; but not always. In many cases learners are rather perceiving, discriminating, understanding or interpreting: processes which also involve a high degree of mental activity.

The two essential characteristics of a good language-practice task are: clear *objectives*, accompanied by the necessity for *active language use* (as defined above).

Objectives

The main task objective is clear and simple, and involves some kind of challenge. Some examples: to solve a problem, to guess something, to get someone to do something, to create some kind of pleasing composition, to brainstorm ideas, to get to know one another. Note that such an objective does not have to be 'authentic' in terms of replicating a possible real-life situation or event. It is enough that it is interesting or fun in itself, and produces learner activity in language use.

Underlying this main objective is the pedagogical one of providing for useful grammar practice: a guessing game produces question forms, getting someone to do something involves the imperative, and so on. In the most successful grammar activities the two kinds of objectives are combined: the non-linguistic one being the main motivating focus, while both teacher and students are aware of the 'secondary', linguistic one (see *Language tips* throughout). The amount of attention paid to each aspect varies: if students get involved in discussing personal feelings while describing past experiences, it obviously will be inappropriate to ask them to concentrate on using the past tense correctly; but if the objective is to produce or edit something for publication, correct usage will be stressed.

In any case, the objective has to be a reasonably simple one that can be defined in a few words, so that students are clear in their minds what they are doing and why. It is very much easier to define an objective if there is a concrete result to be achieved: a list to be written out, a solution to be found and displayed, a story to be narrated, a picture to be drawn or marked. In such cases, it is often more effective to explain the objective in terms of the end product ('Find and write down some solutions to this problem ...') than in terms of the process ('Think about some ways you might solve this ...').

Active language use

The learners are able to attain the objective only by an exertion of effort in some kind of active language use; though this, as noted above, may involve the so-called 'passive' skills of listening and reading. And this active language use provides for repeated exposure to or production of the target grammar point (see *Quantity*, p. 7).

So we need to make sure that the activity is in fact based mainly on using language, and does not waste too much time on mime, colouring, artistic creation or silent brain-racking. This may sound obvious, but it is surprising how many otherwise excellent classroom activities fail to teach much because of such components. It is tempting to think that if students (particularly children) are happily absorbed in doing a task in a language lesson, they are therefore learning the language – but this is not always true. They may, of course, be achieving other equally (or more) important educational objectives, for the sake of which we may opt, temporarily, to forgo the language-learning focus. But normally we want to make sure students are spending their time in profitable language learning.

Sometimes certain rules are introduced that limit how the task objectives are to be achieved, in order to make sure that maximum language use in fact takes place. Take, for example, the objective of finding ten differences between two similar pictures. If you ask learners to do this as a team when they can all see both pictures, they may just circle the differences on their pictures without talking at all. If, however, you limit them with the 'rule' that they may not point to or touch the pictures, then they have to describe them in speech (*10.3 Picture differences, Variation 1*). Such rules have the added bonus that they often make the activity more challenging and interesting (see the next section below).

If we design our task in such a way that it has clear linguistic and non-linguistic objectives, and obliges learners to engage repeatedly with the structure that is being learnt in the process of achieving them, then we have the basis for a good grammar practice activity. But it is only the basis. The students may still not do it very well if they find it boring.

Interest

Learners may, as already noted, be motivated to participate in a learning exercise by *extrinsic* factors that have nothing to do with the nature of the activity itself – they may very much need to know the language in order to pass an exam, for example, or want to perform well in order to win approval. Activity design, however, aims to create *intrinsic* motivation: the desire to participate and learn because of interest-arousing features within the activity itself.

Topic

The (non-linguistic) topic of the activity is usually the first thing that comes to mind when teachers think of factors that arouse interest. However, I have found that this is in practice probably the least important of the features listed here! A boring topic can easily be made interesting by a challenging task; an interesting topic can equally easily be 'killed' by a tedious one. The topic is important in only a minority of the activities in this book; and a lot of the tasks can be adapted to use a wide range of different topics (see, for example, *1.1.4 Adjective poem* or *4.2.2 How will the story end?*).

It is also not true that topics have to be relevant to the students' situations, or provide new information, or be stimulating or exciting: there is no single guideline for the selection of subjects that will arouse learner interest. A more reliable piece of advice is to use different kinds of topic at different times, to make sure that there is a varied 'diet' of subject matter. Here is a selection of some of the kinds of topic used in this book:

- Factual information on topics of general interest: history, geography, psychology, politics, science, etc.
- Controversial subjects of local or general interest
- Personal viewpoints, experiences, feelings, tastes
- Fiction: novels, short stories, anecdotes, folk tales
- Amusing or pleasing ideas as expressed in poetry, proverbs, quotations
- Entertainment: films, plays, television programmes
- Personalities: locally known people, famous celebrities, imaginary characters

However, you will find a lot of the activities use none of these: they are based on boring subjects like telephone numbers (*12.1.1 Telephone numbers*) or familiar objects (*11.2.3 Shopping*): and they arouse and maintain interest through a combination of two or more of the following task-design features.

Visual focus

It is very much easier to concentrate on thinking about something if you can see it, or at least see some depicted or symbolic representation of it. Sight is an extremely powerful and demanding sense: if we do not provide our students with something to look at, they will seek and find it elsewhere, in objects that have nothing to do with the learning task and that may distract them. An exercise that uses both aural and visual cues is likely, therefore, to be more interesting than one that is only aural-based.

A written text may provide sufficient visual focus in itself; but accompanying graphic material often improves comprehension and performance. It can help to elucidate difficult content, add meaning to a very short or boring text, or be used to compare and contrast ('The text says she's dancing, but in the picture she's sitting down.').

Visual material usually takes the form of pictures; but it may of course be a representation of information in some kind of other graphic form: diagrams, symbols, icons, tables, and so on. We ourselves are often an excellent visual aid when using our own facial expression and physical movement to illustrate a topic; so are our students and the classroom environment.

These days we have a variety of different technical means to show visual materials besides the traditional black- or whiteboard: the computer screen sometimes projected through a data projector; the interactive whiteboard; the OHP. But in most classrooms paper is still the most convenient and user-friendly for activities based on group, pair or individual work.

Open-endedness

A task that is open-ended allows for a number of different, equally valid, learner responses, and is therefore conducive to the production of varied and original ideas.

Even if the basic structural framework of the response is prescribed in advance, learners' motivation to participate rises significantly if they are allowed to choose the actual 'content' words to use: the contributions, written or spoken, become less predictable and more interesting. For example, supposing you want to practise adverbs of frequency: one technique is to supply a sentence such as *He has coffee for breakfast*, and then ask students to insert the adverb *always*. The result is boring because it is predictable and of uninteresting content. But if you supply a human subject (even a fairly obvious one like *people*, for example), and ask the students to suggest things that people always (or never, or sometimes, or whatever) do, then you will get a variety of responses, many of them interesting or funny. You will also, incidentally, get substantial *quantity* of practice, as defined earlier. True, this also means that participants have to find their own vocabulary: but if the range of possibilities is wide enough, then usually even less advanced students can find something to say; and you can always supply the occasional new word as needed.

It is not, however, true to say that all closed-ended tasks are boring. When you want to practise certain points of grammar that the learners still have difficulty in producing on their own, there is a place for activities based on very controlled responses; and these can be made more interesting by varying intonation, facial expression and gesture, by the use of visuals, or by introducing game-like features such as competition, time limits, role play and so on (see, for example, *17.1.1 Detectives*).

Information gaps

An *information gap* exists when one person knows something that the other doesn't, and they need to communicate in order to bridge this gap (convey the information). The existence of information gaps should not be taken to be the sole criterion of genuine 'communication': there are many examples of real language use that is obviously communicative in spite of their absence (greetings, for example, or joking repartee). But it is true that the transmission of new ideas from one participant to another does occur in most real language-based transactions; and when this factor is built into a classroom language-learning task, the effect is to add a feeling of purpose, challenge and authenticity which improve learner interest.

For example, learners are often asked to practise the interrogative by taking an answer and reconstructing the question: a useful exercise for sharpening awareness of interrogative forms, but uninteresting at least partly because the content of the answer is known in advance. If, however, students ask each other questions in order to get the necessary information to fill in a form (*7.3.5 Filling in forms*) or engage in a guessing game (*7.1.1 Guessing*), then they are asking questions whose answers they do *not* know in advance, but need in order to perform a task; and their interest in both question and answer is likely to be enhanced.

Personalization

By *personalization* I mean the use of students' own personal experiences, opinions, ideas and feelings.

As an example of a non-personalized exercise, learners can be asked to practise present perfect forms by discussing how long something shown in a picture has gone on or has been going on. This can be a useful, heterogeneous exercise providing plenty of use of the structure. But a much higher level of interest is likely to result if we ask students to talk about things they themselves have done or have been doing (as in *14.3.7 I have lived here for ...*). Their contributions are interesting not only because they are open-ended (see *Open-endedness*, pp. 15–16), therefore unpredictable and likely to be very varied and original, but also because there is an element of personal investment: the students are 'giving' of themselves to each other, and finding out real information about one another. This not only raises the level of attention to what is said, it also tends to contribute to an atmosphere of warmth and friendliness within the class.

There is, of course, a limit to how personalized we can be without becoming intrusive or causing embarrassment or distress; but most teachers are sensitive enough to detect where this limit lies.

Maximum participation

It is important to make sure that all members of the class, or as many as possible, have opportunities to participate in the activity simultaneously. This is one reason why the conventional teacher-student 'ping-pong' interaction is so boring: only one student is activated at a time, and the others are just hanging around with not much to do. In contrast, when all the class are asked to respond simultaneously to something they hear – or when they are engaging in individual work on writing responses to a task – they are all likely to feel involved.

This is one of the reasons why, if the activity allows it, pair work is in principle likely to be more interesting for participants than group work. In group work, one or more of the group members may opt out and get bored, because they are not directly challenged to participate: this is unlikely to happen if they are working in pairs.

For more details on different kinds of classroom activation patterns and resultant levels of participation see *Learner activation*, pp. 19–23.

Game-like features

I do not usually call activities 'games' in the classroom, unless their main purpose is just to have fun. Any procedure whose main objective is learning is by definition a learning activity. However, this does not mean that we cannot use some features of games to increase interest and enjoyment. Serious learning does not mean being solemn; and we have a lot to learn about the nature of enjoyment and interest by looking at what happens when we play games.

Apart from the 'time-out' recreational aspect ('this isn't real life, this is just for fun'), the enjoyment we get from playing games derives from two main components: a clear and (potentially) achievable goal; and some artificial and temporary constraints which are the 'rules' of the game. For example, the goal of tennis is to hit the ball so that your opponent cannot hit it back: but you have to get the ball over the net and within the white lines. The goal of chess is to checkmate the king of your opponent: but you can only move your pieces in certain ways.

Such goals and rules induce a slight feeling of tension, a slight rise of adrenalin in the players, which we all feel when we play games (and sometimes also when we just watch them). And it is this which is the main source of pleasure. This pleasure may be increased or decreased if we 'win' or 'lose'; but winning or losing is itself only the final stage, and does not explain the ongoing pleasure in the process of playing.

A grammar practice activity, then, should be presented to the class frankly as such, but may be made more enjoyable and interesting to do by the introduction of 'rules' that induce the element of pleasurable tension associated with game-playing.

For example, if the class is shown a picture and invited to make up sentences about it using the present progressive, the objective is rather ill-defined, and there is no particular challenge involved. If, however, we edit the objective by introducing a much more clearly defined goal: 'Make up 20 sentences about the picture using the present progressive' – there is an immediate rise in the feeling of challenge ('Can we get to 20 or can't we?'), and interest increases. We can increase it still further by introducing the 'rule' of a time limit ('Make up as many sentences as you can about the picture using the present progressive in two minutes. Start ... NOW!') (see *8.1 Describing pictures*).

Entertainment

Another source of interest is sheer entertainment: the reception or creation of ideas or graphic forms that are in some way aesthetically pleasing or amusing, or both. Listening to stories or songs, or watching films or plays or television programmes can obviously give pleasure; perhaps even more effective for our purposes are those activities where the entertainment is supplied by the students' own contributions.

Exercises that are based on combining or comparing ideas not usually juxtaposed can produce all sorts of amusing results: *9.3 Desert island equipment*, for example, where participants have to find reasons to justify using unexpected and incongruous articles on a desert island. Apparently straightforward brainstorming procedures often produce entertaining contributions: how many things can you think of that you might/could do with a pen?, for example (*9.2 Uses of an object*): students get pleasure from both composing and hearing (or reading) original ideas. More serious, but equally pleasing, results can be obtained from activities like *16.7 Preposition poem* where students work together to compose a poem.

Role playing

Learners often enjoy 'being' someone else, or being themselves in an imaginary situation. And a temporary departure from reality, incidentally, is not only a means of motivating learners to participate, it is also a very effective way of widening the range of language available for use: if the students are acting the roles of explorers in the jungle, or soldiers in an army, or young children arguing with adults, they will be able to use varieties of language not usually appropriate for learners in the classroom.

There is a difference between role play, where each student takes on a particular personality for an individual purpose, and simulation, where the entire group is talking through an imaginary situation. In the latter type of activity, the individuals are usually acting as themselves – but not always: they may be called on to play particular roles, in which case simulation is in fact combined with role play. Either may provide a framework for some excellent grammar practice, both controlled (see, for example, *7.3.1 Dialogues*) and relatively free (*21.1.1. What to do*). Many information-gap and opinion-gap activities can function far more interestingly and effectively if given the added dimension of a simulated non-classroom situation. For example, exchanges based on giving and taking can be given the imaginary context of shopping (*11.2.3 Shopping*); or students can role play the participants in an asking-and-answering activity (*7.3.6 Preparing interviews, Variation 2*).

These, then, are the main ways in which we can arouse and maintain learner interest. However, they will work only if as many members of the class as possible are actively involved as suggested above under the heading *Maximum participation*: which brings us to the next section.

Learner activation

When the activity is based on writing or silent reading, or on listening by all the class to a central source of spoken text, then it is fairly easy to activate all the class simultaneously. The problem arises when we want them to speak, or to participate in some kind of full-class interaction. Many of the activities in this book have students speaking; and most of them conclude with a full-class sharing or summary discussion.

Different classroom activation types produce different types and levels of participation, and it is important to choose the right one to fit the learning objective of the task.

The main types of oral activation in the classroom are the following.

Teacher talk

The teacher talks, students listen.

The usefulness of teacher talk is often underestimated. Teacher talk is extremely useful, if not essential, when, for example, explaining a grammar point before embarking on practice, or when giving instructions how to do an activity. But there are also situations where the teacher him/herself tells a story, describes something, reads aloud a written text: often the teacher can present material in a way that is much more interesting and engaging than the same content heard from a recording or from other students. And such presentations may result in very substantial learning: providing comprehensible further examples of how a grammatical structure is used to make meanings, or models for later student production (see, for example, *14.1.2 Listening to stories*, or *Teaching tip*, p. 32).

Teacher talk + brief student responses

As well as giving the teacher an opportunity to monitor their learning, the necessity to make responses helps learners to concentrate on the exercise as a whole, and focuses their attention on the particular points being taught.

In brief-response activations, the learners are asked to react to what they hear by physical gesture, brief answers or quick written notes: discrimination activities, for example, where the learner picks out specific items or meanings from a listening text (see, for example, *10.7 Discrepancies*), or brief physical or verbal responses to cues (*5.1 Please!*)

'Ping-pong'

The most common kind of verbal interaction in the classroom is the teacher-student 'ping-pong' exchange: the teacher asks a question, a student responds, the teacher approves or corrects. The choral response – where two or more students answer together – is a variation of this. Essentially, the teacher is the focus of attention, and is in full control of learner responses, largely able to determine what these will be, and in a position to monitor them.

This technique is most convenient to use at an early stage in practice when you wish to make sure that the learners are hearing and producing acceptable forms. But later it has serious drawbacks.

- There is usually relatively little language production by the learners compared to the amount of teacher input.
- The cues, each demanding only one response, tend to be geared to a single level, thus not providing very useful practice for less, or more, advanced members of the class.

- Since each such exchange is 'closed' to participation by other members of the class, they often do not bother to listen to each others' responses, and another potential source of learning is lost.

This kind of interaction, therefore, is of limited use in grammar practice.

Student–teacher exchanges

A variation of the above is a sort of 'reverse ping-pong', where the student initiates the exchange, and the teacher (or some other central 'responder') replies. This is a useful technique which is rarely used – perhaps because teachers do not like to forgo the initiative! Its advantage is that while the teacher can still monitor learners' utterances and provide good models of acceptable grammar, the learners themselves can decide on the content, and initiate their own ideas. Because of the originality of their contributions, students tend to listen to each other much more than in the conventional 'ping-pong' described above. This technique is particularly good for practising interrogative forms (*7.3.6 Preparing interviews*).

Brainstorm

Another more productive variation of the 'ping-pong' type of interaction is the brainstorm. Instead of asking a conventional closed-ended question with one right answer, the teacher gives an open-ended cue which has any number of possible answers, and several students can respond. The teacher talks less, the students more, and a far higher proportion of the class is involved in the interaction. The stimulus may be a question with plenty of possible answers (see, for example, *2.2.2 What do you do when ...?*); or a picture to be described, commented on or asked about (*8.1 Describing pictures*); or a phrase or brief text that can be expanded in different ways (*3.1 Finishing conditional sentences*); or a problem demanding diverse solutions (*9.8 Dilemmas*).

Chain responses

As in a brainstorm, instruction and an initial cue are given by the teacher, resulting in a large number of responses by the learners. The difference is that whereas in a brainstorm all these responses relate to the original cue, in a chain only the first does, and thereafter each learner utterance is made in response to the one before. The simplest form of this is question-and-answer: A asks B a question, B answers and then asks C something, using the same, or a parallel, formula:

A: What do you like doing in your free time, B?
B: I like dancing. What do you like doing, C?
C: I like playing tennis. What do you like doing, D? ...

This technique produces a high proportion of learner talk, while allowing the teacher to monitor. There is usually some flexibility of response, giving students a chance to express individuality (*14.1.4 Chain story*).

A variant is the 'cumulative chain', where each student has to repeat all the previous contributions in order, before making his or her own addition (*11.2.2 Piling up stores*).

Fluid pairs

The basic idea for a transaction-based exchange between two students is provided by the teacher, often in the form of a prescribed dialogue. Each learner performs only one transaction with any one partner, and then goes on to do it again with another. For example, in a beginner class, the simple dialogue:

A: Do you have ...?
B: Yes, I do. Here you are. / No, I'm sorry, I don't have any.

is used by 'buyers' and 'sellers' in a shopping simulation, as the 'buyers' move around trying to acquire the different items on their lists (*11.2.3 Shopping*).

If the information provided in the exchange is based on individual tastes or opinions, then the same question will produce different answers with different people, so there is some point in asking it again. Some 'fluid pairs' activities, for example, are based on doing a mini-survey (*17.1.4 Opinion questionnaires*): learners go from one to another of their classmates to find out the answers to their questions.

The fluid-pair technique provides an extremely useful framework for repetition – with a communicative purpose – of set questions or exchanges. It is not used very often: possibly because of the fear by teachers that the large amount of verbal interaction between students and physical movement will result in class management problems. In my experience, however, students doing a fluid-pair exercise very rarely deviate from the task they have been set – though admittedly they can be very noisy: it is a good idea to have a bell or some other prearranged signal for stopping.

Pair/small-group discussions

The teacher provides a clear, simple task which is to be done in pairs or small groups. The language to be produced by students can be semi-controlled (they are told to make use of certain patterns or kinds of sentences), but the exact content is left up to them. Usually such transactions are based on an information-gap task. For example, students may give each other directions or commands (*16.5 Describe and arrange*), or convey or request specified information (*21.1.1 What to do*).

Freer discussions in pairs or small groups are appropriate for students with a fairly good mastery of the language. The teacher gives a task whose performance is likely to involve use of the grammatical structure being practised and simply lets the students get on with it, with minimum intervention. Because of the relative lack of teacher control over what is said, this model is best used at the stage where the learners can be relied upon to produce acceptable forms of the structure in prescribed or controlled contexts, and when you want to give them experience in using it more naturally and spontaneously in their own self-initiated speech.

What they will actually say is up to the learners themselves: in theory, they may choose not to use the structure you want them to practise at all! But it is possible to design the discussion task in such a way that they are in fact very likely to do so; for example, a discussion task based on discussing experience relevant to a present situation is likely to produce the present perfect (*14.3.6 The right experience for the job*).

Most of the above interaction types have obvious parallels in reading and writing tasks: a task based only on a written text, for example, would also involve learners in reading very much in the same way as *teacher talk* involves the learners in listening. Question-and-answer exercises can be modelled on *teacher talk + brief student responses, ping-pong, brainstorm*, and so on. However, when engaged in the 'silent' skills (reading/writing/listening), the choice of interaction type is less significant: all participants can be activated simultaneously regardless of the type of elicitation; whereas in tasks involving speech, the type of interaction makes a crucial difference.

Many of the activities in this book in fact provide 'integrated skills practice' (they combine listening and speaking with reading and writing). But where there is spoken interaction, the activation is predominantly based on types which elicit a relatively high proportion of student participation.

Practical tips

In this section I will suggest a few brief tips for getting the most out of the activities shown in *Part 2* of this book.

Check if you need to do any preparation.
If there's no 'Preparation' heading at the top of the activity, that means you don't need to prepare anything: but if there is, then make sure that you have in fact got everything ready!

Give instructions **before** putting the students into groups.
If the class is to do any kind of independent (individual, group or pair) work in the process of the activity, it is vital for the instructions to be clearly given before they start. I have often seen teachers put students into groups and then start explaining, with the result that students often don't listen: many of them already have their backs to the teacher, and they are distracted by each other. The result is likely to be that the teacher has to stop the activity in the middle to repeat instructions, or that there is delay and a constant distracting buzz of talk as students consult each other to try to work out what they have to do.

Give instructions **before** giving out written material.
Where the activity is based on some kind of worksheet, the same applies. Giving out the material before you explain often results in students starting to read it instead of listening to your instructions. And again: they then don't know what to do, and you often find yourself having to explain again.

Show bits of the text on the board and explain what to do with it; then, when you've finished and are sure they all understand, distribute the material.

Give instructions in the students' L1 (if feasible).
In many classes where everyone shares the same language it can be really helpful to explain what the task is in that language (unless, of course, the class is advanced enough to cope easily with explanations in the target language). If you give instructions in the target language, then a) many students may not understand, and b) the whole process takes longer – at the expense of time you could use for doing the activity itself.

Some teachers do first one and then the other: target language followed by L1 translation. This is not a very good idea: it takes even longer, and students very quickly learn that they don't need to listen to the target language explanation, because the L1 version is coming up shortly.

Run a rehearsal.

If the task is to be done in pairs or groups, supplement your explanation with a brief full-class 'rehearsal' of the task. Choose some of your more confident students, and act out a sample task with them in front of the rest of the class to show how it works.

This is probably the best way of clarifying what is to be done, particularly when a task is multi-stage or difficult to explain.

Tell them how it will end.

The instructions for an activity based on independent (individual, group or pair) work should usually include some provision for ending. Tell the students how long the activity is expected to last, what they should do after they finish, what happens if some finish early or late, what is to be done with any written or recorded results.

It's very useful to have some kind of signal – a bell or tambourine, for example, or turning the lights on and off – to indicate when everyone should stop and come together for some kind of summing up.

Make the language-learning aim explicit.

Usually it is a good idea to be frank about the language-learning aim: 'Try to guess what I have in my bag – but I'll only accept correct questions, because we're practising questions here.' Or even: 'We're going to do the following activity in order to practise ... (whatever). Here's what we're going to do.'

There are various reasons for this. The first is honesty: however authentic or game-like the task, it is in fact a grammar practice activity, and the students should be aware of the fact. Second, it is desirable in principle to let students know what the teaching/learning aims are at any point in the course. Third, most activities will simply work better if the goals are shared by both teacher and learners. Finally, adult learners are sometimes unwilling to participate in what may seem to them trivial play unless they understand the serious learning benefit that will result.

Help them get it right.

I have already discussed the principle of 'success-orientation' (pp. 7–8). The contribution of the teacher during the activity, by the same principle, has to be mainly helping the learners to get it right, rather than just giving the task and withdrawing. Examples of such assistance are: simply giving extra time to reread or think; repeating or simplifying a text; approving the beginning of an utterance in order to encourage production of the whole; suggestions, hints, prompts. All this means that we have to be very alert to sense when and where help is needed (and when it is not!), and what form it should take. And there is a wider educational message: I, the teacher, am here to help you, the learner, succeed and progress in your learning, not to judge, scold or make you feel inferior.

Give homework.

Homework is a useful way of extending classroom exercises, of giving an opportunity to review the material, of practising in reading and writing what has been done only orally in class and vice versa. This is probably homework's primary function; a secondary one is to serve as an informal test, providing the teacher with useful feedback as to how well the material has been mastered.

Very often suggestions listed under *Variations* or *Follow-up* can furnish the basis for homework assignments.

You will find further practical tips on specific types of activities or language problems scattered throughout *Part 2* under the headings *Teaching tip*, *Language tip* and *Language and teaching tip*.

PART 2 Activities

1 Adjectives

1.1 ADJECTIVE BEFORE THE NOUN

1.1.1 Guessing adjectives

Focus	Position of the adjective before the noun
Age	Any
Level	Elementary
Time	10–15 minutes
Preparation	10 or 15 slips of paper with adjectival phrases written on them (see *Box 1.1.1*)

Procedure

1 One student gets a slip, which he/she does not show anyone.

2 The student tells the others only what the noun is: they have to guess the entire phrase. For example, if the 'knower' gives the noun *table*, the others might guess:

> A square table?
> A small table?
> A wooden table?

3 If they can't guess, the knower may give a hint: the first letter of the adjective, for example, or a general hint like 'It's a colour'.

Variations

1 Students work in small groups round a table, with a pile of such slips face down in the middle of the table. They take turns picking up a slip and saying the noun; the others guess the adjective-noun combination.

2 Later, students think up their own combinations for guessing. Remind them that such combinations should be reasonably rational and 'guessable' (not 'a red elephant', for example!).

Note

Insist on the students using the entire phrase when making their guesses. Just saying 'big?' or 'young?' gives no practice in the adjective-before-noun construction.

Box 1.1.1: Guessing adjectives

A tall man	A fat baby	A brown cow
A happy girl	A small computer	A beautiful picture
A white dog	A young student	A long story
A soft bed	A red light	A black book

1.1.2 Inserting adjectives

Focus Position of the adjective(s) before the noun
Age Any
Level Any
Time 5–10 minutes
Preparation Make one copy of a short text or extract from a text (not more than 100 words or so), with any adjectives that were in the original text deleted (by hand).

Procedure

1 Tell the students you are going to read out the text slowly: they have to raise their hands to stop you any time they think they can insert an adjective.
2 Read the text aloud. Accept any suggestions for adjectives as long as they make sense, but make sure students say the whole phrase ('a large house'), not just the adjective ('large') (see *1.1.1 Guessing adjectives, Note*).
3 Every time students insert an adjective, start reading again from the beginning, inserting the adjectives they have previously contributed as you read. Ask students to help you remember which adjective went where!

Variation

Give students a typed-up double-spaced copy of another text with its adjectives deleted, but no obvious gaps left where they are missing. Challenge students to insert adjectives – as amusing and original as they can. Later, they read out their different versions to the class.

Note

You may wish to provide a set of adjectives in advance for students to choose from; this makes the procedure easier but lessens its heterogeneity and interest.

1.1.3 The same tastes

Focus	Position of the adjective(s) before the noun
Age	Any
Level	Elementary–Intermediate
Time	10 minutes
Preparation	A copy of Table A (see *Box 1.1.3a*) for each student

Procedure

1. Give the students Table A.
2. Tell them to imagine they are small children and their parents have told them they can choose one kind of pet. Each student circles one option in each column to show which kind of pet they want.
3. Each student tries to find someone else with the same choices by asking others. For example:

   Do you want a big white cat?

   (See *Fluid pairs*, p. 22.)
4. The search process goes on until most of the students have met and talked to each other.
5. In full class, ask who found one or more people with similar tastes.

Variation

Use one or both of the other tables. In Table B, the situation is that the students have enough money to buy one of each kind of item shown: what would they like to buy? In Table C, they are simply exchanging information about their tastes in books, music and films.

Note

If you use Table C, draw students' attention to the way nouns such as *adventure* and *crime* can be used like adjectives in English. They might be able to use such words in the next activity, *1.1.4 Adjective poem*. If you want more practice on this point, look at *11.5.1 A business school.*

Box 1.1.3a: The same tastes

Table A: What pet do you want? I want a …

big	black	dog
small	brown	pony
fat	white	cat

Box 1.1.3b: The same tastes

Table B: What would you like to buy? I'd like to buy some …

modern	French	paintings
old	Spanish	vases
colourful	Italian	glasses

Box 1.1.3c: The same tastes

Table C: What kinds of novels/music/movies do you like? I like …

<table>
<tr><td>crime</td><td rowspan="3">novels,</td><td>classical</td><td rowspan="3">music</td><td rowspan="3">and</td><td>adventure</td><td rowspan="3">movies</td></tr>
<tr><td>romantic</td><td>folk</td><td>science fiction</td></tr>
<tr><td>modern</td><td>pop</td><td>funny</td></tr>
</table>

1.1.4 Adjective poem

Focus	Adjectives after *is/are*; position and order of the adjectives before the noun
Age	Teenager–Adult
Level	Intermediate–Advanced
Time	15–20 minutes
Preparation	A sample adjective poem (see *Box 1.1.4* for an example) shown on the board and/or copied for students

Procedure

1 Show the students the sample poem.

2 Explain the pattern:

Line 1: Noun
Line 2: Noun + *is/are* + adjective
Line 3: Noun + *is/are* + adjective, adjective
Line 4: *Is/are* + adjective, adjective, adjective
Line 5: Adjective, adjective, adjective, adjective
Line 6: Noun.

3 Students choose their own topics, compose their poems, copy them out neatly and then read them out.

> **Language tip**
>
> It might be worth taking some time out to talk about the order of series of adjectives before nouns. Remind students to put opinion words (e.g. *good, bad, lovely)* before descriptive ones (e.g. *big, green, soft*). For more detailed guidelines, see Swan (2005, p. 11).

Follow-up

Later, students may be invited to write out their compositions artistically (perhaps using computer graphics) and post them on the classroom noticeboard or website.

Box 1.1.4: Adjective poem

Fog
Fog is scary
Fog is scary, wet
Is scary, wet, thick
Scary, wet, thick, cold
Fog.

Teaching tip

When a student has composed something that is to be displayed or read out to the rest of the class, it's a good idea to read it out yourself rather than making the student do so. You can probably make it sound much more fluent and impressive than he/she can (and you can correct mistakes as you go!). It is also a subtle compliment to the student to have his/her work read out by the teacher.

1.2 COMPARISON OF ADJECTIVES

1.2.1 Adjectives on the Internet

Focus	Comparative of adjectives: recognition and understanding (Variation: superlative of adjectives)
Age	Any
Level	Elementary–Intermediate
Time	20–30 minutes
Preparation	You will need an online computer for each student or small group.

Procedure

1 Brainstorm as many adjectives as the class can think of (up to about 30), and write them on the board.
2 Each student selects one of them and writes down its comparative form.
3 They Google™ this form and find five different contexts in which it is used. These must be a) clearly understood and b) interesting or funny.
4 Each student presents his/her most interesting example. Who has found the funniest or most original contexts?

Variation

Do the same with the superlative form.

Notes

1 It's fine for two or more students to choose the same adjective if you don't have enough to go round. The results are likely to be different anyway.
2 If you don't have enough computers, students can be asked to work in pairs or threes. Or they can do the main task for homework, printing out their results and reporting back to the class the following day.

1.2.2 Brainstorming comparisons

Focus	Comparative and superlative of adjectives; *(not) as ... as ...*
Age	Any
Level	Elementary–Intermediate
Time	15–20 minutes

Procedure

1 Write on the board the names of three objects (or animals, or occupations, or whatever you like (see *Box 1.2.2a* for some examples)), and ask students to find as many points of comparison between the items as they can. For example, if they are given *a hammer*, *a walking stick*, *a pencil*, they might say:

A pencil is smaller than a hammer.
A walking stick is longer than a pencil.
A hammer is the heaviest.
A hammer is not as useful as a pencil.

2 Select another set of items from *Box 1.2.2a* (or ones you think up yourself), and write them up on the board.
3 Students work in pairs or small groups. Which group can find and write out the most comparisons? Note that these have to be written out as sentences by a 'secretary' – it's not enough just to write an adjective!
4 Stop the work after ten minutes, and elicit results.

Variations

1 A similar task can be set for individual writing or for homework.
2 Use the same nouns in the plural to give practice in plural sentences.
3 You can do the same with (captioned) pictures (see *Box 1.2.2b* for some examples). This means enlarging or projecting the pictures onto the board for the full-class stage and then making copies for students for the group-work stage. But then the comparisons should use the definite article ('the castle', 'the caravan'), as they are relating to a particular depiction, not to castles and caravans in general.

4 If students know each other fairly well, they can work in pairs and compose sentences comparing themselves with each other. For example:

You are taller than me.
Your hair is longer than mine.

Language tip

It's quite acceptable to say 'than me' rather than 'than I' in the context of informal conversation. But in formal writing, it would be preferable to say 'than I' or 'than I am'.

Box 1.2.2a: Brainstorming comparisons

- a pencil, a walking stick, a hammer
- an elephant, a snake, a mouse
- a television, a laptop, an MP3 player
- a pool, a sea, a river
- an apple, a mango, a banana
- a motorcycle, a car, a bus
- football, chess, computer games
- (local foods)
- (popular television programmes)
- (well-known personalities)

Box 1.2.2b: Brainstorming comparisons

a castle

a caravan

a cottage

a family car

a racing car

a black cab

a baby

a boy

a woman

a doctor

a firefighter

an astronaut

1.2.3 Bigger, better, faster!

Focus	Comparatives and superlatives in advertising slogans
Age	Any
Level	Intermediate–Advanced
Time	15–20 minutes

Procedure

1 Ask the class if they know of any advertising slogans that use comparatives or superlatives (if they only know of ones in their own languages, elicit or provide translations). Examples in British English include *Farmers Weekly*'s 'Local food is miles better' and men's toiletry firm Gillette®'s 'The best a man can get'.

2 With the class, create a slogan using a comparative or superlative form of an adjective to promote something they all know about – the school itself, a local food or a public event – and write it up on the board.

3 Invite students to work in pairs creating a new slogan for any product, event or facility they know about, using comparative or superlative forms of the adjective. These can later be displayed on the class noticeboard or website.

Follow-up

The slogan may later be developed into a full advertisement, written out and decorated (perhaps in the form of a web page), or into a television commercial, to be acted.

Note

This activity can be used to practise any form of comparison; but you can, of course, limit it to one particular type if you wish when you give the preliminary instructions: the comparative with *-er than*, for example, or the form *(not) as ... as ...*

1.2.4 Circle comparisons

Focus	Comparative of adjectives; *(not) as ... as ...* (Variation: superlative of adjectives)
Age	Any
Level	Elementary–Intermediate
Time	5–10 minutes

Procedure

1 On the board, show the students several nouns laid out in a rough circle as follows:

pasta
salt apples
yoghurt ice cream
water curry
fish

The nouns should be connected in sense to a common theme (see *Box 1.2.4* for more examples).

2 Ask students to suggest a point of comparison between any two. For example:

Ice cream is more fattening than yoghurt.
Yoghurt has fewer calories than ice cream.

3 Draw a line between 'ice cream' and 'yoghurt' to represent the link, and ask for another sentence linking two other items, and so on, until there is a criss-cross of lines linking the words.

Follow-up

1 Point to one of the lines, and challenge the class to remember what sentence it represented. If they succeed, delete the line. Continue until all the lines are deleted.

2 For homework, students may be given sets of nouns on paper to work on individually, drawing in the lines and writing the corresponding sentences below.

Variation

Ask the students to say which is *the ... -est* or *the most ...* of all the items in the circle. Draw a circle round the item they have selected. Go on until all the items have been circled (if possible!); some items may be circled more than once.

Box 1.2.4: Circle comparisons

boots
sandals
a coat
jeans
a shirt
a hat

a lion
a fish
a spider
a mouse
a snake
a cat

reading
studying
swimming
dancing
watching TV
playing computer games

a hairdresser
a movie star
a bus driver
a doctor
a pilot
a mechanic

a cup
a teaspoon
a plate
a bowl
a knife

a submarine
a ship
a yacht
a Windsurfer™
an aircraft carrier
a raft
a rowing boat

Language tip

Strictly speaking, *fewer* should be used with count nouns ('fewer calories') and *less* with non-count ('less time'). But in fact many people use *less* with count nouns as well ('less students in the class'), and this usage is becoming acceptable.

1.2.5 Preferences

Focus	Comparative (and superlative) of adjectives to express personal preferences
Age	Teenager–Adult
Level	Intermediate
Time	20 minutes

Procedure

1 Present two words expressing concepts that are likely to arouse positive or negative reactions (see *Box 1.2.5* for some examples: use the first two only of each set).

2 Assign one area of the classroom to each of the concepts, and invite students to go to the area which represents the one they prefer.

3 Invite students to exchange ideas with others in their area about their preferences, using the following sentence-stem as a base:

I prefer _____ because they are / it is _____ -er / more _____.

For example:

I prefer lakes to waterfalls because they are quieter.

They may then go on to add further details, not necessarily using the comparative.

4 They then meet students from the opposite 'group' to exchange opinions.

5 Tell everyone to sit down, and elicit in the full class some of the ideas that came up. Share your own preferences as well. What do most people prefer, and why?

Variations

1 The same can be done with three (or four) concepts instead of two (add the third (and fourth) item of each set in *Box 1.2.5*), in order to elicit the superlative. For example:

I prefer lakes because they are the quietest.

2 Each student chooses his or her own pair or set of 'concepts' and goes round asking all the others which they prefer and why. In this way, all students are activated simultaneously, either asking or answering in a 'fluid pair' procedure. They can be asked to draw conclusions as to the tastes and reasons of the majority, which may be interesting to share with the rest of the class at the end.

Note

You might use for the basic concepts things you have been studying recently in class: new vocabulary, characters from stories you have read, etc.

Box 1.2.5: Preferences

- lakes, waterfalls, the sea
- green, red, blue
- dogs, cats, canaries
- morning, afternoon, evening
- summer, winter, spring, autumn
- swimming, dancing, running
- sweet, savoury, spicy food
- pop, classical, folk music
- the guitar, the trumpet, the violin
- silk, cotton, wool

1.2.6 Which is heavier?

Focus	Questions and answers using the comparative and the superlative
Age	Any
Level	Intermediate
Time	10–15 minutes
Preparation	Copies of sets of questions based on comparisons (see *Boxes 1.2.6a* and *1.2.6b*)

Procedure

1 Students get copies of one of the quizzes and work in pairs to write in the answers. If, for example, the question was 'Which is the highest mountain in Africa?', they may write the short answer 'Mount Kilimanjaro'.

2 In a full-class feedback session, ask: 'What's the answer to number one?' Students then have to answer in full sentences. For example:

Mount Kilimanjaro is the highest mountain in the Africa.

Follow-up

For homework, students make up as many questions as they can on the same model. They can use websites such as http://www.guinnessworldrecords.com/.

Box 1.2.6a: Which is heavier?

Comparatives

1 Which is heavier: a kilo or two pounds?
2 Where are there more people: in Indonesia or in Japan?
3 Which is the larger country: Russia or China?
4 Who can expect to have a longer life: a man or a woman?
5 Which has less iron: a banana or an orange?
6 Which can jump the longer distance: a kangaroo or a horse?
7 Which country produces more rice: China or India?
8 Which is bigger: a Boeing 787 or an Airbus A380?
9 Which ocean is deeper: the Atlantic or the Pacific?
10 Which is faster: a horse or a bicycle?
11 Which is heavier: a kilo of feathers or a kilo of gold?
12 Which animal has fewer stripes: a tiger or a zebra?

Box 1.2.6b: Which is heavier?

Superlatives

1 Which is the highest mountain in Africa?
2 Which weighs the least: the brain of a human, a polar bear or a dolphin?
3 Which is the largest planet in the solar system?
4 Which animal has the longest life?
5 Which is the longest snake in the world?
6 Which planets have the fewest satellites?
7 Which country produces the most wheat?
8 What is the shortest word in the English language?
9 What is the lowest lake in the world?
10 Which is the fastest land animal in the world?
11 What is the lightest gas?
12 Which is the brightest star in the sky?

Variation
Invite students to compose quizzes using comparatives and superlatives about members of the class or about local personalities, places or events.

Note
These quizzes also provide practice in *fewer/fewest, less/least* and *more/most* as the comparative and superlative forms of the determiners *few/little* and *much/many* (for example, 'more people').

Answers (Boxes 1.2.6a and 1.2.6b)

a Comparatives

1 a kilo 2 Japan 3 Russia 4 a woman 5 an orange
6 a kangaroo 7 China 8 an Airbus A380 9 the Pacific
10 a bicycle 11 they are the same 12 a zebra

b Superlatives

1 Kilimanjaro 2 a polar bear 3 Jupiter 4 the tortoise
5 the python 6 Mercury and Venus (they have none) 7 China
8 I 9 the Dead Sea 10 the cheetah 11 hydrogen 12 Sirius

1.3 ADJECTIVES AFTER *BE* OR OTHER COPULAR VERBS

1.3.1 Guessing by description

Focus	Adjectives after *be* or other copular ('linking') verbs
Age	Any
Level	Beginner–Elementary (or Intermediate, for the Variation)
Time	10–15 minutes

Procedure
1 Describe an object to the class, using *is* and adjectives, and ask the class to guess what the answer is. Tell them, for example:

It is round.
It is sweet.
It is green, or sometimes red or yellow.
It is hard.

– the answer being 'an apple'.

2 Put students in pairs or groups, and invite them to invent similar definitions for other objects for you and the rest of the class to guess.

Variations

1 Do the same with verbs of sense (another type of copular verb). For example, the 'apple' definition above could run:

> It feels smooth and hard.
> It tastes sweet or sometimes a bit sour.
> It looks attractive.
> It smells slightly sweet.

2 For homework, ask students to write similar definitions for three objects of their choice, which you then have to guess.

1.3.2 Not what it seems

Focus	Adjectives after copular verbs
Age	Teenager–Adult
Level	Intermediate–Advanced
Time	20–25 minutes

Procedure

1 Give students the first half of a sentence which includes a copular verb followed by an adjective, such as:

> It doesn't taste very nice, but …
> He seems attractive, but …

and ask them to think about how the sentence could end and what it might refer to. For example:

> … it will help you get well. (Answer: medicine)
> … in fact he's very dangerous. (Answer: a villain from a movie)

2 Write on the board a number of possible copular verbs, such as *look, appear, seem, sound, taste, smell, feel.*

3 Invite students in pairs or small groups to think of further items which are not what they seem. They should write for each a sentence similar to the examples you have given, using as many as possible of the verbs on the board in the different sentences.

4 Representatives of the pairs or groups read out the sentences: the rest of the class try to guess what the subject was.

2 Adverbs

2.1 MANNER ADVERBS

2.1.1 How can you do it?

Focus	Manner adverbs as modifiers of verbs
Age	Any
Level	Elementary–Intermediate
Time	5–10 minutes

Procedure

1 Suggest any verb or verb-based phrase the class have learnt recently, and write it in the centre of the board. For example, 'drive a car'.

2 Challenge the students to find at least 10 adverbs that could go with the verb using the sentence base 'You can ...'. They might, for example, suggest:

You can drive a car fast.
You can drive a car dangerously.
You can drive a car carefully.

3 Write up the adverbs in a circle round the verb as the students suggest them.

4 If they easily reach 10, raise the challenge to 20!

Variations

1 Having done this once or twice in the full class, divide pupils into pairs or small groups, and give them the basic verb / verb phrase and two or three minutes to suggest adverbs. Pool results: which group found the most?

2 This can be done the other way round: suggest an adverb, and ask students what actions could go with it. What actions can be done 'carefully', for example?

Note

Students may suggest rather incongruous adverbs. For example:

You can drive a car gracefully.

Demand that they justify their suggestions and describe when such sentences might be appropriate!

2.1.2 Miming adverbs

Focus	Manner adverbs and their position in the sentence
Age	Young–Teenager
Level	Elementary–Intermediate
Time	10–15 minutes
Preparation	A list of manner adverbs appropriate to the level of the class (see *Box 2.1.2a* for some examples)

Procedure

1 Select a manner adverb, and tell all the class but one what it is: for example, 'slowly'. The one who does not know gives a command to the other students. For example:

Open your books!

2 If the adverb chosen has been *slowly*, then the students will do the action slowly.

3 The student who gave the command tries to guess the adverb, using a full sentence. For example:

You opened your books slowly.

4 If he/she cannot guess, then he/she gives another command ... and so on until either he/she guesses the right answer or gives up and has to be told!

5 If he/she has to be told, elicit the full sentence in the past from a member of the class. For example:

We opened our books slowly.

> **Language tip**
>
> Note that if there is a direct object in the sentence, many languages insert the adverb immediately before it, leading to mistakes like *'We opened slowly our books'. Hence the importance of eliciting responses in full sentences.

Variations

1 The command can be given to a single individual instead of to the entire class: this is quieter and perhaps quicker but lowers the amount of student participation.

2 Instead of using real, classroom-based actions for the commands, use more imaginative ones that can be mimed: for example, 'climb a tree', 'clean a window' (see *Box 2.1.2b* for some examples).

Box 2.1.2a: Miming adverbs

Elementary

- angrily
- carefully
- gently
- happily
- hungrily
- noisily
- quickly
- quietly
- sadly
- seriously
- slowly

Intermediate

- anxiously
- busily
- calmly
- cautiously
- dramatically
- elegantly
- fearfully
- lazily
- nervously
- politely
- silently
- thoughtfully

Box 2.1.2b: Miming adverbs

- Climb a tree!
- Clean a window!
- Catch a ball!
- Put on a hat!
- Say 'Hallo'!
- Eat an apple!
- Wave goodbye!
- Open a suitcase!
- Pick a flower!
- Put up a picture!

2.2 FREQUENCY ADVERBS

2.2.1 Frequency surveys

Focus	Position of frequency adverbs before the verb
Age	Any
Level	Elementary–Intermediate
Time	20–30 minutes
Preparation	Copies of the 'frequency' questionnaire (see *Box 2.2.1a*)

Procedure

1 Give out the copies of the questionnaire, and go through the text making sure all questions and instructions are understood. Make clear what you mean by *always* (every day?), *sometimes* (twice a week? twice a month? every other day?), etc., otherwise students may have difficulty deciding what to answer.

2 Students fill in the first column of their own questionnaires about themselves.

3 Students ask each other the questions, and fill in their classmates' responses (in the other column(s)).

4 When everyone has filled in at least one further column, tell them to return to their seats.

5 Elicit reports of results in full sentences. For example:

I always watch television at weekends.
Sam never watches television alone.

Variations

1 Use the questionnaire on teachers in *Box 2.2.1b*.

2 Compose your own questionnaires – or invite students to do so – on other habits that may interest your class: food and eating, leisure-time activities, sleeping, computer use, mobile phone use, travel.

Follow-up

1 Ask students to write five or six full sentences in their notebooks, either in class or for homework, describing selected interesting results of their questionnaire.

2 Ask the students how many people answered 'always' to the first question, how many answered 'very often' ... and so on, so that you can get a general idea of what most people in the class do!

Box 2.2.1a: Frequency surveys

Television-watching habits
By each question fill in a letter:
A = always B = often C = sometimes D = rarely E = never

How often do you . . .	Name:	Name:	Name:
1 . . . watch television on a weekday?			
2 . . . watch television at the weekend?			
3 . . . turn the television on automatically when you come home?			
4 . . . feel guilty about watching too much television?			
5 . . . look up programmes before turning the television on?			
6 . . . watch programmes alone?			
7 . . . turn the television off if visitors come?			

Box 2.2.1b: Frequency surveys

A good teacher I have known
By each question fill in a letter:
A = always B = often C = sometimes D = rarely E = never

How often did he or she . . .	Name:	Name:	Name:
1 . . . give homework?			
2 . . . play games?			
3 . . . make jokes?			
4 . . . give punishments?			
5 . . . praise students?			
6 . . . criticize?			
7 . . . get angry?			
8 . . . smile?			

Now fill in the table again for *A bad teacher I have known*!

2.2.2 What do you do when …?

Focus Position of frequency adverbs before the verb
Age Any
Level Elementary–Intermediate
Time 5–10 minutes

Procedure

1 Ask students a cue question like, 'What do you do when you are feeling down?' (see *Box 2.2.2* for some examples), and ask them to jot down a few ideas, using one of the frequency adverbs *always*, *usually*, *often*, *sometimes* each time. For example:

I sometimes go out and buy some new clothes.
I usually just sit and listen to music.

2 Invite them to share ideas with each other and later with the full class.

Follow-up

Use their ideas as a basis for a discussion about what kinds of thing lots of people do in certain situations, or what kinds of thing are really helpful to ease a negative situation.

Box 2.2.2: What do you do when …?

Moods:

What do you do when …

- … you are feeling down?
- … you are happy?
- … you are annoyed?
- … you are bored ?
- … you are nervous?
- … you are tired?

Situations:

What do you do when …

- … you have a free day?
- … you have an exam the next day?
- … you have too much to do?
- … you can't sleep?
- … someone is rude to you?
- … you can't find your keys?
- … you have quarrelled with a friend?
- … you are short of money?

3 Conditionals

3.1 Finishing conditional sentences

Focus	Conditional sentences of the type *If* + present followed by *will* (Variations *If* + past followed by *would/could*)
Age	Any
Level	Intermediate
Time	10–20 minutes

Procedure

1 Provide half a sentence, beginning *If* ... followed by a present tense. For example:

If I get home early today, ...

(See *Box 3.1a* for some examples.)

2 Provide an example of how you might complete the sentence yourself:

I'll do some gardening.

3 Tell each student to think of his/her own ending and write it down (faster workers should write more than one).

4 Elicit different ideas from the students.

5 Do the same with other *If* ... beginnings.

Variations

1 Do the same using the form *If* + past tense (see *Box 3.1b* for some examples).

2 Do the same but the other way round, starting with the 'result' clause ('I will go on vacation if ...', 'I would talk to him if ...'). (See *Box 3.1c* for some examples.)

Follow-up

If the activity is done in full class, students may later try to recall what other students' variations were. For example:

If Mario gets home early today, he'll watch his favourite programme on television.

After hearing a few suggestions, ask students to recall:

What were the most interesting endings you heard?
Who remembers what Monique would do?

Box 3.1a: Finishing conditional sentences

If I get home late tonight, …
If I can't sleep, …
If I have time next weekend, …
If I get a high grade in my next exam, …
If you come to my home, …

Box 3.1b: Finishing conditional sentences

If I had a million dollars, …
If I were not here, …
If I could have one wish, …
If I had 20 children, …
If I had a museum, …

Box 3.1c: Finishing conditional sentences

***will* + if**
I will be very disappointed if …
It'll be great if …
I'll help you if …
I will be very surprised if …
We'll solve the problem if …
***would* + if**
We would all learn English much better if …
I'd have more energy if …
I'd be very happy if …
I would buy a new car if …
We'd take a day off if …

Teaching tip

You may wish to use the terms 'first conditional', 'second conditional' and 'third conditional' when using these activities. The first conditional refers to sentences with *if* + present tense followed by *will*, the second conditional to *if* + past followed by *would* and the third conditional to *if* + past perfect followed by *would have*.

3.2 Chains of events

Focus	Conditional sentences of the type *If* + past, followed by *would* (Variations: other types)
Age	Teenager–Adult
Level	Intermediate–Advanced
Time	20 minutes

Procedure

1 Give the class one *if* clause (see *Box 3.1b* for some examples). For example:

If I had a million dollars, ...

2 One student suggests a possible result. For example:

If I had a million dollars, I would go round the world.

3 The next student takes the result, re-forms it into a condition and suggests a further result, and so on. For example:

A: If I had a million dollars, I would go round the world.
B: If I went round the world, I would meet some interesting people.
C: If I met some interesting people, I would write a book about them.
D: If I wrote a book, I would become famous.

Variations

1 The same can be done using other types of conditional. For example:

A: If I am ill tomorrow, I'll stay at home.
B: If I stay at home, I'll miss lessons ...

or:

A: If the car had been going faster, it wouldn't have been able to stop in time.
B: If it hadn't stopped in time, it would have caused an accident ...

Supply new vocabulary as needed.

2 Each student gets a sheet of paper, at the top of which he or she copies down the given *if* clause (or each student may be given a different one or invent their own). The student then fills in a possible result and passes the paper to a neighbour, who thinks of and writes down the next event in the chain (using full conditional sentences as in the example given for oral work above) and passes it on. After about ten minutes there will be a number of 'chains' ready to be read aloud or put up on the wall.

Language tip

You'll probably need to teach students that it is correct to say *If I/he/she **were*** instead of ***was***. But note that this usage is tending to decline today: more and more you hear people saying: 'If I was ...', 'If she was ...'.

3.3 Superstitions

Focus	Conditional sentences of the type *If* + present, followed by *will*
Age	Teenager–Adult
Level	Intermediate
Time	10–15 minutes

Procedure

1 Suggest some superstitions well-known to the students, defining them through conditional sentences. For example:

If you walk under a ladder, you will have bad luck.

If the sky is red in the evening, it will be a fine day tomorrow.

(See *Box 3.3* for more examples.)

2 Students are invited to suggest further superstitions they know, which may be written on the board or copied down. They will probably need some new vocabulary; supply as needed.

3 Students should feel free at any stage to comment on suggested superstitions and to add variations that they know about.

Notes

1 Students might find it a little difficult at first to recall superstitions, though they probably know many if reminded. You may need to jog their memories ('What about the one about black cats?'). It is also a good idea to ask them to think of superstitions they know for homework the night before, writing them out as conditional sentences or even simply making brief notes which can be expanded in class. They can Google™ 'superstitions' to find more ideas.

2 Superstitions may be a sensitive subject, as some may carry religious or personally significant implications, so be aware of possible student reactions, and select items for discussion carefully.

Variations

1 In a multilingual/multicultural class, ask students to tell the class about superstitions from their own culture.

2 Students write up their favourite superstition on a large sheet of paper or poster and display in class.

Box 3.3: Superstitions

- If you walk under a ladder, you will have bad luck.
- If the sky is red in the evening, it will be a fine day tomorrow.
- If you break a mirror, you will have seven years' bad luck.
- If there is a bee in your house, you will receive a visitor.
- If you see a small spider, you will get a lot of money.
- If you see a coin and pick it up, you will have good luck all day.
- If your left hand is itchy, you will give money away.
- If you touch wood, your good luck will continue.
- If you catch the bride's flowers when she throws them at her wedding, you will get married soon.
- If a black cat crosses your path, you will have good luck.
- If you put shoes on a table, you will have bad luck.

3.4 Justifying actions

Focus	Conditional sentences of the type *If* + past, followed by *would/could*
Age	Teenager–Adult
Level	Intermediate–Advanced
Time	20–25 minutes

Procedure

1 Suggest a set of four or five unlikely actions, displayed on the board or dictated, and ask students in pairs or groups to think of justifications for doing them. See *Box 3.4* for some examples. For example:

Why would you …

… jump out of the window?

… refuse an invitation to a friend's party?

2 Students try to think of circumstances in which they might perform these actions and write them down. For example:

> If the house was on fire, and if I could not get to the door, I would jump out of the window.
>
> If I didn't like the people going to my friend's party, I might refuse the invitation.

(Note that the responses do not have to use the exact words of the initial cue.) Students should try to make do with vocabulary they know, without asking you for new words.

3 After a limited time – five or six minutes, during which you too write down your own suggestions – students and you share ideas.

Note

The modal *might* can naturally be used in this context: 'Why might you ...?', and the response 'I might ... if ...'. *Might* is an alternative to *would* if the action is only a possibility rather than a fairly likely option.

Teaching tip

When an activity involves thinking up creative responses to cues, as in many of the activities in this book, it's important not to demand instant responses, but to give a few minutes for students to think of ideas and perhaps write them down before starting a full-class 'sharing' session.

Follow-up

1 Small-group discussions may be held on the basis of students' suggestions in order to decide on the most convincing possible reason (the *if* clause) for each course of action (the 'result' clause). Groups then compare their results with each other, and possibly decide together on the 'best' answers.

2 The cues may be used as the basis for creative writing, but in this case students should be encouraged to describe more details or to add further suggestions as to circumstances which would justify the action.

Box 3.4: Justifying actions

Why might you ...

- ... jump out of the window?
- ... burn (paper) money?
- ... deliberately break a glass?
- ... pretend to be someone else?
- ... drive a car on the wrong side of the road?
- ... stop eating for two days?
- ... smile at someone you don't know?
- ... eat a piece of paper?
- ... not answer an email?
- ... sit on the floor?

3.5 Looking back

Focus	Conditional sentences of the type *If* + past perfect, followed by *would/could have*
Age	Teenager–Adult
Level	Intermediate–Advanced
Time	25–30 minutes

Procedure

1 Students are told to write down (using the past tense) three events that they are glad about (positive) and three that they regret (negative). Provide examples from your own experience. For example:

Positive: My family moved to this town.
Negative: I never knew my grandmother.

2 Tell the students what it would have meant to you if things had been different. For example:

If my family had not moved to this town, I would never have met my husband.
If I had known my grandmother, I would have been able to hear about her life when she was young.

3 Invite students to write down their own three ideas for each category (Positive/Negative) and what would have happened / not have happened if things had been different. Supply new vocabulary to individuals as needed.

4 Afterwards, students share and discuss experiences in small groups. Each participant in turn chooses one item to talk about. Other participants

should be encouraged to respond to the stories, ask about them and share similar or different experiences.

> **Teaching tip**
>
> When you are going to elicit any kind of personal response from a student (memories, opinions, feelings), it helps a lot if you start off by providing a similar contribution of your own. Students will be more confident and willing to share their own personal responses if they know you are doing the same – as well as, of course, getting a model of the grammatical point in context!

Follow-up

An essay title can be given such as *Why I regret* ... or *Why I am glad I* ... You may wish to direct students to use conditional sentences in their essays, but these would be likely to occur anyway if the essay is given as a follow-up to the classroom activity described in the procedure.

3.6 I wish ...

Focus	*I wish* to express unfulfilled desires; conditional sentences of the type *If* + past, followed by *would/could* (Variation 1: *If only* to express unfulfilled desires)
Age	Teenager–Adult
Level	Intermediate–Advanced
Time	15–20 minutes

Procedure

1 Tell the students to imagine they are to be given three wishes and to write down what these would be. For example:

    I wish I could speak English fluently.

  They should then add a reason using *If* + past, followed by *would/could*:

    If I could speak English fluently, I would be able to travel more.

2 Check, as far as you can, that their sentences are correct.

3 Students then get together in small groups and share their wishes and reasons for them.

Variations

1 You might use 'If only ...' as an alternative to 'I wish ...'.

2 An amusing variation is to ask students to write down three negative wishes – things they would hate to do, or hate to happen to them – possibly using the formula *I would hate it if* ... For example:

I would hate it if I lived at the North Pole.

Then the procedure follows that described above.

4 Future tenses

4.1 FUTURE WITH *GOING TO*

4.1.1 Mickey's diary

Focus	*Going to* to express future plans (Variation 2: *will be doing*)
Age	Adult
Level	Elementary–Intermediate
Time	30–40 minutes
Preparation	Copies of a diary showing the days of the week filled in with notes of different planned activities (see *Box 4.1.1*)

Procedure

1 Students read through the diary and discuss what kind of a person Mickey is. Man or woman? (Could be either: they decide.) Family? What's his/her job? (Various possibilities!)

2 Students suggest how some of the notes in the diary could be expanded to full sentences. For example:

    Mickey is going to be in the office from 9 am on Thursday.

3 Each student adds one new imaginary appointment or plan to Mickey's diary, in brief note form as in the original (for example 'Shopping').

4 Students get together in groups and tell each other what the additions are. They explain these in full sentences. For example:

    Mickey is going to do the shopping on Monday afternoon after the office.

  The other students insert the entries in brief note form on their copies of the diary.

Variations

1 The same can be done for some of the entries using the present progressive with future meaning ('Mickey is flying to London'). Note, however, that this doesn't work with entries involving *be*: these would stay with *going to* ('Mickey is going to be in the office').

2 To practise *will be ...ing*, ask the students questions like: 'What will Mickey be doing at 3 pm on Tuesday?'

Box 4.1.1: Mickey's diary

12 MONDAY	13 TUESDAY	14 WEDNESDAY
7.00	7.00	7.00 Fly to London
8.00	8.00	8.00
9.00 In the office	9.00 In the office	9.00 AT HOME
10.00	10.00	10.00
11.00	11.00	11.00
12.00	12.00	12.00
13.00 Lunch with Tony to discuss new project	13.00 Leave for airport	13.00 In the office
14.00	14.00	14.00 Discuss Irish trip with boss
15.00	15.00 Fly to Dublin	15.00
16.00	16.00	16.00
17.00 Leave the office	17.00 Meeting with Irish colleagues	17.00 17.30 Leave the office
18.00	18.00	18.00 Family time
19.00	19.00 Dinner at Trinity College	19.00
20.00	20.00	20.00
21.00	21.00	21.00

PHOTOCOPIABLE

15 THURSDAY	**16** FRIDAY	**17** SATURDAY
7.00	7.00	Morning 10 am Take boys to football practice 10.30 Coffee with Kit
8.00	8.00	
9.00 In the office	9.00 In the office	Afternoon 15.30 – 16.30 Tennis with Kit, Max, Carol
10.00	10.00	
11.00 –11.45 Meeting with the team	11.00	
12.00	12.00	Evening 19.00 Party at club
13.00	13.00 Lunch with boss to talk about new project	
14.00	14.00	**18** SUNDAY
15.00	15.00	Morning Gardening
16.00	16.00	
17.00 Leave the office	17.00 Leave the office	Afternoon
18.00	18.00 Supper at Mum and Dad's	
19.00 Restaurant with Pat	19.00	
20.00	20.00	Evening
21.00	21.00	

Follow-up

1 After the students have worked for a while on the diary, collect it and challenge them to reconstruct as much as they can of the diary from memory. Write up the seven days of the week on the board, leaving a space beneath each for notes. One student might remember, for example:

Mickey is going to fly to Dublin at 3 o'clock on Tuesday afternoon.

You write up the appropriate note on the board. When you and the class together have filled in everything you can remember, redistribute the original and see what you've forgotten!

2 The same can be done in groups, sharing results at the end.

4.1.2 Finding a time to meet

Focus	*Going to* or present progressive to express future plans
Age	Teenager–Adult
Level	Elementary–Intermediate
Time	25–30 minutes
Preparation	Copies of blank diary tables (see *Box 4.1.2*)

Procedure

1 Give students the blank diary tables, and tell them to fill in at least 12 imaginary plans. These can be expressed very briefly, e.g. 'Shopping' or 'Football'. (This bit can be done for homework if you wish to save class time.)

2 Students meet in pairs to find a time when they are both free to meet by saying, for example:

What are you doing / going to do on Thursday morning?
I'm going to play football.

or:

Can we meet on Thursday morning?
Sorry, I'm playing football then.

3 When they find a time they are both free to meet, they write each other's name in the appropriate cell. They then repeat this process with another partner. This continues until all students have fixed at least four meetings or until they are unable to find anyone to meet in the little spare time remaining.

Box 4.1.2: Finding a time to meet

	Mon	Tues	Wed	Thur	Fri
Morning					
Afternoon					
Evening					

4.1.3 Future of a picture

Focus *Going to* or *about to* to describe imminent action
Age Any
Level Elementary–Intermediate
Time 10–15 minutes
Preparation A picture of some kind of interesting or dramatic action shown on the board or copied for students (see *Boxes 4.1.3a–f*, or use suitable material downloaded from the Internet)

Procedure

1 Display one of the pictures, and ask the class: 'What do you think will / is going to happen next?', or 'What do you think is about to happen?'

2 Students contribute suggestions, using *going to* (or *about to*). They should get at least six suggestions for each picture shown. Provide new vocabulary as needed.

Variation

Usually this activity takes the form of a free brainstorm; but sometimes there may be a 'right' answer – if, for example, the picture is taken from a movie and you know what comes next; or if the picture is one of a series (e.g. one of those in *Boxes 14.1.3a–d*) with the sequel available. Then the activity may take the form of a guessing-game, and you can help with hints ('Look carefully at his face, and think again!' ... 'You're very close!').

Follow-up

For homework, several such pictures may be given, and the students write a sentence for each; or one picture may serve as stimulus for a full paragraph.

Box 4.1.3a: Future of a picture

Box 4.1.3b: Future of a picture

Box 4.1.3c: Future of a picture

Box 4.1.3d: Future of a picture

Box 4.1.3e: Future of a picture

Box 4.1.3f: Future of a picture

4.1.4 Mime continuation

Focus	Interrogative of *going to* to ask about imminent action
Age	Any
Level	Elementary–Intermediate
Time	15–20 minutes
Preparation	A set of cue-cards or slips of paper, on each one of which is written a sentence using *going to*, describing an action about to be done (see *Box 4.1.4*)

Procedure

1 One student takes a slip and mimes things he or she might do leading up to the future action. The mime should not, of course, include a demonstration of the action itself!

2 The others have to guess what is about to happen, trying to get as near as possible to the text of the cue-card by asking, for example:

   Are you going to drive a car?
   Are you about to drive a car?

Variation

Students think up their own future actions to mime. You should have a reserve supply of ideas ready to help the less imaginative or confident ones.

Box 4.1.4: Mime continuation

You are going to drive a car.	You are going to wash your face.
You are going to drink a cup of tea.	You are going to talk to a friend.
You are going to play a guitar.	You are going to shout.
You are going to fall asleep.	You are going to listen to music.
You are going to pick a flower.	You are going to play football.
You are going to paint a picture.	You are going to dance.

4.2 FUTURE WITH *WILL*

4.2.1 Future of an object

Focus	*Will* to describe non-imminent future events
Age	Any
Level	Intermediate–Advanced
Time	15–20 minutes

Procedure

1 Suggest a simple object or raw material – an egg, for example – and ask students what they think *will* happen to it in the future. For example:

It will be part of a cake.
It will fall on the floor and break.

2 Give groups of students lists of five or six such items (see *Box 4.2.1* for some examples), and ask them to note down possible future destinies for each one: as many as they can think of within the vocabulary they know. Ideas are noted down by a 'secretary'.

3 All the ideas for each item are compared or pooled in the full class: which object/material is the most versatile?

Box 4.2.1: Future of an object

a stone	a piece of plastic sheeting	a sheet of glass
a potato	an egg	a microchip
a handful of cotton fibre	a spring	some steel wire
a piece of wood	a bag of sugar	a cardboard box
a screw	a litre of water	a chain
a few grains of sand	an orange	a bottle
a bunch of grapes	a diamond	a carton of milk
a bar of iron	a roll of paper	a joint of meat

Language tip

In formal speech or writing, people sometimes use *shall* with the first person singular or plural; but it's increasingly common these days to use *will* with all persons. With pronouns, it's quite normal to use the contracted *'ll* form in speech and all but the most formal writing.

4.2.2 How will the story end?

Focus	*Will* (or *going to*) to describe future events
Age	Any
Level	Intermediate
Time	5–20 minutes
Preparation	Any story appropriate to the students' level, but without its ending, or with an uncertain or ambivalent ending

Procedure

1 Tell the incomplete story, and invite suggestions as to how it will continue.

2 You may disclose the 'right' ending (if there is one) at the end of the activity – or adopt one of the students' suggestions – or approve them all.

Note

The fact that the story is to lead to suggestions for further action in the future tense does not necessarily mean that it has to be told in the present; it is quite acceptable to use the past tense in the narrative and then use the future to discuss possible sequels.

Variations

1 The activity may be made a little longer and more varied by stopping the story at several different points as it goes on, not just at the end. You may read a long story in instalments, stopping at exciting points to ask the class what they think will happen next (continuing later); or a film, a recorded narrative or a play may be halted occasionally to give opportunities for conjecture.

2 For those who teach literature as part of the English syllabus, this procedure can be used when presenting a story, play or novel for the first time to stimulate discussion of plot or character ('Judging from what you know of X's personality, how do you think she will react when she finds out ... ?' 'Do you think this is going to end happily or tragically?' 'Why?').

> **Teaching tip**
>
> It's usually advisable to tell the class stories in your own words rather than reading them out (unless, of course, the students are following the text in their books). This is partly because while telling the stories yourself, you can maintain eye contact with the class, adapt to their language level and insert brief explanations or translations as necessary. Also, it's nearly always easier to understand any speech if it's generated 'on line' by the speaker rather than read aloud from a written text.

4.2.3 Horoscopes

Focus	*Will* to predict future events
Age	Teenager–Adult
Level	Intermediate
Time	20–30 minutes

Procedure

1. Give the students ten minutes to compose a horoscope for next week for another student in the class (they don't know who) on a loose sheet of paper. It should be not more than 50 words long, interesting and not too serious (see *Box 4.2.3* for some possible beginnings).
2. The papers are folded, collected and placed in a bag.
3. Each member of the class then takes, at random, a piece of paper which is to be his or her 'horoscope', and reads it. Some or all of the 'horoscopes' may be read aloud.

Notes

1. For students unfamiliar with the idea of a horoscope, you may need to explain what it is and possibly show them an example from an English-language newspaper or magazine.
2. The idea of horoscopes may not be acceptable to some religious groups, so check before using it.

Variations

1. Ask the students to compose very optimistic and desirable horoscopes. Then, instead of distributing them personally, put the horoscopes up on the wall round the class. You and the students then go round reading them – and correcting the English, if necessary – and each member of the class chooses one future he or she would like and appends his or her name at the bottom. They may choose more than one.

2 Ask students to compose an ideal horoscope for themselves and another for someone (anonymous!) they don't like; or one for a specific person – you, a fellow student, a famous politician or television personality.

Follow-up

A week later, ask the students if anything predicted in their horoscope actually came true. Can they recall the actual wording of the original prediction?

Box 4.2.3: Horoscopes

- You will get a letter / a text message / an email saying ...
- You will meet someone who ...
- You will have a ... experience/surprise.
- You will have some problems with ...
- You will solve a problem which ...
- Someone will tell you ...
- A good friend will ...
- Your plans will ...

4.2.4 The world tomorrow

Focus	*Will* to predict future events
Age	Teenager–Adult
Level	Intermediate
Time	10–20 minutes

Procedure

1 Ask students to write down a list of changes they expect to see in the world by a date 50 years in the future. For example:

We'll have a working day of four hours.
Every home will have a video telephone.

2 The ideas are then read out and discussed. Those that most of the class agree with may be written up on the board.

Variations

1 You may find it helpful to give the students a series of topics (education, technology, politics, fashion, sport, health, the environment), and ask them to write one or more ideas for each. Or adult students may each select an area they feel expert in and describe three or four developments they expect to occur in these areas.

2 Ask students to predict changes in their own lives in, say, ten years' time. For example:

I'll be married with three children!

3 In groups, students can try to sort their predictions into 'optimistic' and 'pessimistic' ones – not always as clear-cut a distinction as you might expect!

4.3 THE FUTURE PERFECT TENSE

4.3.1 By six o'clock

Focus	The future perfect with *by* + time expression
Age	Any
Level	Intermediate–Advanced
Time	10–20 minutes

Procedure

1 Tell students what you will have done by six o'clock this evening, and what you won't have done by that time. For example:

By six o'clock I'll have come home from work, but I won't have had supper.

2 Ask them to tell each other in pairs, or write down, what they will and won't have done by six o'clock.

3 Share in the full class.

Follow-up

Provide students with a few variations of the time expression –

by next Thursday
by tomorrow morning
by December
by next year

– and ask them to suggest things they will or won't have done by then.

5 Imperatives

5.1 Please!

Focus	Simple imperatives
Age	Young
Level	Beginner–Elementary
Time	5–10 minutes

Procedure

1 Give the students simple commands. For example:
   Please stand up!
   Please put your hand on your head!

2 They must obey these commands only if you say 'Please!' first; if you omit the 'Please', they should ignore them.

3 Any student who performs a command that was said without 'Please' loses a 'life'. They have three lives, after which they are 'out' and sit down.

4 Stop the procedure after about half the class are 'out', and congratulate those still on their feet.

5 Start again with the entire class.

Note

You may know this as the game 'Simon Says' and may prefer to use the traditional form rather than that suggested here. My version substitutes 'Please' for 'Simon says' as a more useful – and more polite! – alternative.

Variations

1 Add occasional 'Don't' commands!

2 Omit the 'Please' rule; instead, give a simple command, and at the same time do an action which may or may not correspond to it. The students have to do what you **tell** them, not (necessarily) what they see you do.

3 Ask a student to be the one to call out the commands.

> **Teaching tip**
>
> The problem with any game where participants are 'out' if they make mistakes, from the language-practice point of view, is that after they are 'out', they stop participating. An alternative is to let them try to remember, or mark down, how many times they made a mistake, but carry on participating. Then have a feedback session at the end, congratulating those who made no, or few, mistakes.

5.2 Directions

Focus	Imperatives to tell someone how to get somewhere
Age	Any
Level	Beginner–Elementary
Time	15–20 minutes
Preparation	Copies of the map (see *Box 5.2*). Review or teach appropriate vocabulary such as *turn left/right, go straight on, cross the road, stop, along, across, as far as, first/second left/right, traffic lights/signals, roundabout, corner, building, river, road, street, crossroads.*

Procedure

1. Put students in pairs, with their maps hidden from one another. Student A decides where he or she would like to live (on the map), marks the site and directs Student B how to get there from *Start*.
2. Student B then does the same for Student A.

Follow-up

1. Students take it in turns to choose what else they will have in 'their' town (shopping centre, bus station, cinema, etc.), and to direct each other to the site: but they have to go back to *Start* every time they give directions. At the end, they compare maps to check their sites correspond, and compare with other pairs to see how many different facilities are boasted by the different towns.
2. Each student has a map and sticks it into their notebook. They then describe in writing how to get to their 'home'. Take in the notebooks, see if you can understand where their home is from the directions and mark it on the map.

Variations

1 One student gives directions; other students follow them and have to say where they are at the end.
2 Students tell each other how to get to their real homes from where you are at the moment.
3 One student chooses a place not too far from where you all are at the moment and describes how to get there. Other students have to identify what the place is. The same thing can, of course, be done in writing.

Box 5.2: Directions

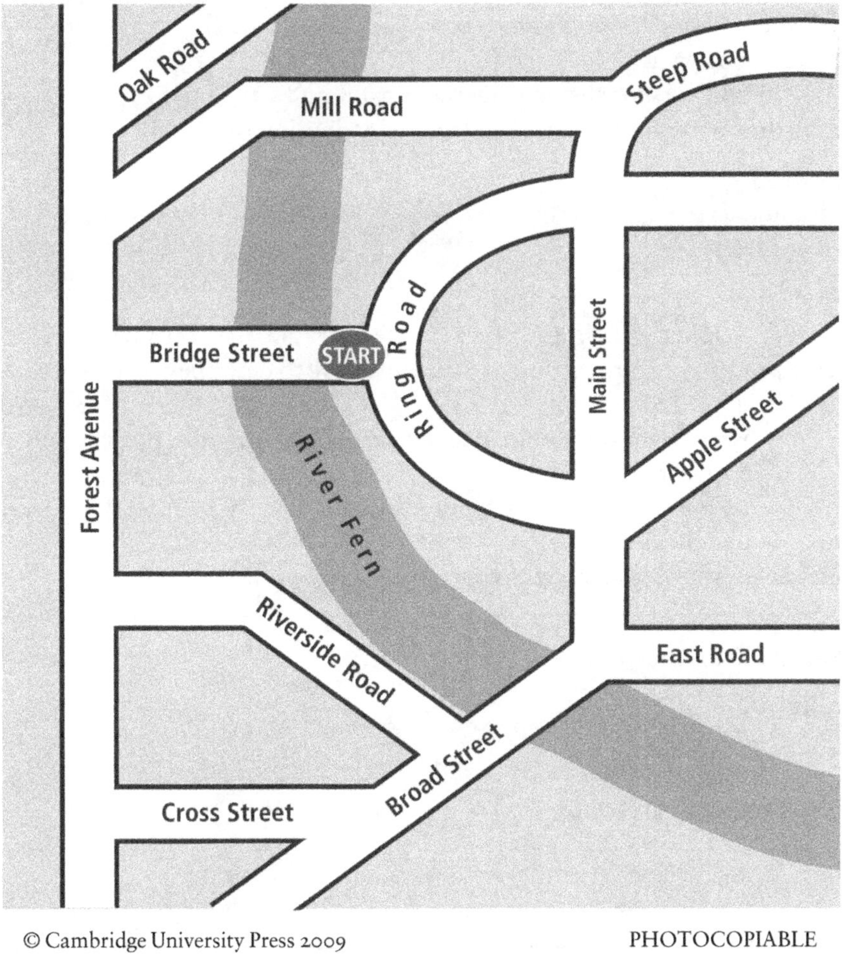

5.3 Recipes

Focus	Imperatives to give instructions in writing
Age	Any
Level	Elementary–Intermediate
Time	30–40 minutes
Preparation	Make sure the students know simple recipe verbs such as *take, add, mix, heat, boil, bake, spread.*

Procedure

1 Tell the class to write out instructions for a simple recipe you specify: making a cup of tea, for example, or a simple local dish (see *Box 5.3a* for some examples). Supply new vocabulary as needed. They may work in pairs if they wish.

2 Invite students to tell you what they wrote, and write up the whole recipe on the board, based on the students' contributions.

Follow-up

Ask students to write out their favourite recipes. Perhaps extend this to a class recipe book!

Variation

Ask for a detailed 'recipe' for a very simple operation, like opening a door (see *Box 5.3b* for some examples): students have to describe everything that has to be done. For example:

> Walk to the door, stop in front of it, turn the handle, push or pull the door open ...

This can be done orally: students give the instructions, you or other students mime or actually do the actions as told.
Alternatively, ask students to write out the instructions on paper.

Box 5.3a: Recipes

How to ...

- ... boil an egg
- ... make a cup of tea
- ... make a cup of coffee
- ... make a salad
- ... make soup
- ... make a sandwich

Box 5.3b: Recipes

How to ...

- ... open a door
- ... send a text message on a mobile phone
- ... wash a cup
- ... cross the road
- ... get money from a cash point

5.4 Dos and don'ts

Focus	Positive and negative imperatives to give advice
Age	Any
Level	Elementary–Intermediate
Time	20–25 minutes

Procedure

1 Ask each student to think of something he or she is good at or knows how to do. It could be a sport, an occupation or a hobby.

2 Tell them to think of pieces of advice for someone else who needs to learn this skill. For example, I might write about teaching:

  Learn your students' names as soon as possible.
  Don't talk too much.

3 Elicit a few examples from students; then ask them each to write at least five positive and five negative pieces of advice for their own area of expertise.

4 Then they get together in pairs or groups to advise each other on, or find out about, their different areas of expertise. This may, of course, develop into an informal discussion, and the brief commands may be elaborated into more detailed recommendations.

Variations

1 Ask the students to work out a list of the best 'dos' and 'don'ts' for a new student or teacher coming to the school, or for someone studying for an exam, or for someone wanting to progress in English.

2 Invite students to think of completely misleading advice to give a tourist coming to visit their country or a student joining the school. For example:

  When you get on an underground train, shake hands with everyone in the carriage.
  Sing the national anthem at the beginning of every lesson.

5.5 Symbols

Focus	Positive or negative commands or invitations
Age	Any
Level	Elementary–Intermediate
Time	15–25 minutes
Preparation	The symbols (see *Box 5.5*) shown on the board or copied for students

Procedure

Ask students to tell you what each symbol is telling you to do, or not to do. For example:

Stop!
Go left!

Variations

1 Download other signs (from the Highway Code site, for example, http://www.direct.gov.uk/en/TravelAndTransport/Highwaycode/Signsandmarkings/index.htm) and ask students to identify the appropriate commands.

2 Invite students to find further command or prohibition signs on the Internet and say what they mean.

Teaching tip

An activity has added value if it can actually provide real information or useful advice, as in 5.4 *Dos and don'ts*, 5.5 *Symbols* and 5.6 *Suggestions*. Remember to relate to the real-life truth and usefulness of students' suggestions as well as to their grammatical accuracy!

Answers (Box 5.5)

1 Stop	11 Park here
2 Don't drink the water	12 Smoke here
3 Wash your hands	13 Cross the road here
4 Don't smoke	14 Go left
5 Pass either side	15 Put out campfires
6 Be careful (danger!)	16 Drive slowly
7 Camp here	17 Go/walk
8 Switch off mobile phones	18 Don't take photographs
9 Don't drink this	19 Wait here for the bus
10 Don't go faster than 20 kph	20 Don't run

Box 5.5: Symbols

5.6 Suggestions

Focus	*Let's / let's not* to make suggestions
Age	Any
Level	Elementary–Intermediate
Time	15–20 minutes

Procedure

1 Suggest a situation which demands some kind of action, and tell the class to imagine themselves in this situation as a group. For example:

You are lost in a strange town.

2 Ask students to make suggestions, beginning with *Let's*, as to what they should do. For example:

Let's look at a map!
Let's ask someone!
Let's find a police officer!

3 They should also make at least one suggestion as to what *not* to do. For example:

Let's not panic!

4 Put the class into small groups, and give them a new situation (see *Box 5.6* for some examples) and three or four minutes to think of similar suggestions (both positive and negative) based on this new situation.

5 Pool the ideas on the board, and decide which are the most important or practical suggestions.

Box 5.6: Suggestions

- You are lost in a strange town.
- You were on a trip and have missed the last bus back to town.
- You are at home and bored.
- You are all on holiday at a hotel and can't sleep.
- Your homework is too difficult.
- You are feeling nervous about a test tomorrow.
- You have all passed the test with excellent grades.
- Your friend has just had a baby.

6 Indirect speech

6.1 INDIRECT STATEMENTS AND QUESTIONS

6.1.1 Can you remember what they said?

Focus	Indirect statements and questions
Age	Any
Level	Intermediate–Advanced
Time	15–20 minutes

Procedure

1 About halfway through the lesson, tell students, in pairs or individually, to note down everything they can remember that anyone has said during the lesson up to now: teacher or students. For example:

Why are you late?
What's the time?
I don't understand.

2 Then ask them to tell you in indirect speech what was said. For example:

Marcia asked Tony why he was late.
Evan asked what the time was.
Donna said she didn't understand.

3 For each suggestion, write up the **name** of the speaker only on the board.

4 Challenge the students to remember what each person whose name is on the board said (some, of course, may have said several things); again, this should be in indirect speech.

Variation

Provide different circumstances as the basis for recalling. For example:

Can you remember what was said last lesson?
Can you remember something that was said in the news recently?
Can you remember what was said in a story you read?
Can you remember what was said in a movie extract we saw?

6.1.2 Reporting interviews

Focus	Indirect statements and questions in writing
Age	Teenager–Adult
Level	Intermediate–Advanced
Time	30–45 minutes

Procedure

1 Invite a volunteer student to the front of the class, and interview him or her for two or three minutes (about a hobby, for example, or an interesting experience, or a future plan).
2 Students listen and take notes.
3 In groups, they then combine the information from their notes and write out as many as they can remember of the questions and answers in indirect speech.
4 Groups join and compare their accounts to see what they had forgotten to report.

Note

By careful selection of topic, you can get students to concentrate on practising a specific tense within the indirect speech clause. For example, an interview about future plans will produce sentences like:

She said she *would visit* New York.

One about past experiences will produce:

He said he *had been* in great danger.

Variations

1 Invite a guest to the classroom, and interview them, or ask students to do so.
2 For homework, ask students to interview someone outside the class on a specific topic agreed on in advance – for example, their views on smoking, fashion or a topical event – and then report results in indirect speech. The interview itself may be conducted in the students' L1 if you are teaching in a non-native speaking environment, as long as the reporting is done in the target language.

6.1.3 Correspondence

Focus	Indirect questions and statements in writing
Age	Any
Level	Intermediate–Advanced
Time	30–40 minutes

Procedure

1 Put students into pairs of 'correspondents'. They should not be sitting next to one another.

2 Each correspondent writes a question on a piece of paper to his/her partner. For example:

 Are you enjoying this course?
 What are you doing after school today?

3 The notes are delivered, and the addressees then answer the question (on the same piece of paper), ask another, linked question and send the note back.

4 This goes on until several lines of correspondence have been put together.

5 After a few minutes, tell the students to stop writing and summarize the correspondence in an indirect speech version. For example:

 Anna asked me if I was enjoying this course. I answered that it was all right, and asked ...

6 Take in the completed reports for checking. In the next lesson, pick out some of the more entertaining, and invite the authors to read them aloud, or do so yourself (see *Teaching tip*, p. 32).

Variation

The correspondence process can be carried out electronically, using 'chat', email or text-messaging.

> **Teaching tip**
>
> The problem with activities based on students writing in response to things written by others is that because they write at different speeds, you get pauses when some students are waiting for others. It's important to warn them about this before the activity starts, and/or provide some other work for them to be getting on with while they are waiting.

6.1.4 People used to believe ...

Focus	Indirect past statements contrasted with present
Age	Teenager–Adult
Level	Intermediate–Advanced
Time	20–25 minutes

Procedure

1 Introduce the topic of the advance of scientific knowledge, and give some examples of what people used to believe:

People used to believe that the world was flat.

and contrast them with:

But now most people know that the world is round.

2 Ask students to think of some more examples of contrasts between past and present beliefs, and write up on the board only the second half of each ('But now most people know/believe/think that ... ').

3 When you have a list of seven or more such items on the board, ask students to recall, orally or in writing, what the first half was ('People used to believe ...').

Variation

Suggest that students recall their own youthful different beliefs or misconceptions ('I used to believe that ...') and share them with one another.

Language tip

One thing you'll notice in some of these activities is that the structure called 'indirect speech' does not necessarily report actual spoken discourse. It's very often used after verbs like *know, think, understand, wonder, doubt*, i.e. representing thought processes. It may be worth drawing your students' attention to this point.

6.1.5 Need to know

Focus	Indirect questions in the present
Age	Any
Level	Intermediate–Advanced
Time	10–15 minutes

Procedure

1 Ask the class what they think a new student needs to know on entering the present course/school; suggest they use the question words *who/where/how*, etc. For example:

> You need to know where the secretary's office is.
>
> You need to know when to come to class.

2 Write up their ideas on the board.

Variations

1 They might add things that you *don't* necessarily need to know!

2 Ask each student to think of a field of activity he or she knows something about – his or her occupation, a hobby, an aspect of his or her way of life – and make a quick list of things someone new to it needs to know. If you are taking up sailing, for example, you need to know how to swim. They share their knowledge with each other.

3 If the students are working in pairs or groups, the listeners may, of course, contribute or criticize. For example:

> Don't I need to know ...?
>
> Why do I need to know that?

A discussion may develop.

6.2 INDIRECT COMMANDS

6.2.1 They told me

Focus	Indirect commands and requests, positive and negative
Age	Any
Level	Intermediate–Advanced
Time	30–40 minutes

Procedure

1 Each student makes a list of four or five people in their lives who they feel influence them, or have influenced them in the past: parents, for example, teachers, friends, 'significant others'. Do the same yourself.

2 Opposite each name, they and you write one thing that they remember this person telling or asking them to do. For example:

My mother: Clean your room.
My friend: Don't forget me.

3 Provide an example from your own experience, and describe it in an indirect command sentence:

My mother was always telling me to clean my room.
My friend asked me not to forget him.

Add further details if you wish!

4 In groups or in full class, students tell each other about these requests, expressing them similarly as indirect command sentences.

5 They add further comments, ask and answer questions and share experiences.

Note

A useful introductory phrase to teach here is '... was always telling/asking me ...' to indicate that the request was something the person made often or regularly.

Teaching tip

Sharing personal experiences can be very motivating and interesting for all concerned, but we have to be careful not to intrude on private 'space'. Make it clear that students don't have to answer questions about their own lives if they don't want to.

6.2.2 What's she telling him?

Focus	Indirect commands and requests
Age	Any
Level	Intermediate–Advanced
Time	20–30 minutes
Preparation	The set of pictures of individuals interacting (see *Boxes 6.2.2a–f*) shown on the board or copied for students

Procedure

1 Take one of the pictures, and discuss what one character is telling/asking the other to do. For example:
  She's telling him to work harder.
  She's telling him not to be late.

2 Then ask each student to select any picture and write down what he or she thinks the speaker is telling or asking the other character to do. If they finish quickly, they should go on to another.

3 Invite one student to say their sentence, and the rest of the class guess which picture the sentence refers to.

4 Find out what other students thought was being said by the same character. (You'll be surprised at the variation in answers!)

5 Invite another student to suggest another sentence, and repeat stages 3–4 above until you have discussed all the pictures. (Stop earlier if you find the process is getting tedious.)

Note

It helps to provide the students in advance with a few useful verbs to be used here: *order, tell, ask, request, invite, advise, beg.*

Follow-up

Invite students to say what the response of the other character(s) will be.

Box 6.2.2a: What's she telling him?

Box 6.2.2b: What's she telling him?

Box 6.2.2c: What's she telling him?

Box 6.2.2d: What's she telling him?

Box 6.2.2e: What's she telling him?

Box 6.2.2f: What's she telling him?

7 Interrogatives

7.1 'YES/NO' QUESTIONS

7.1.1 Guessing

Focus	'Yes/no' questions for guessing
Age	Any
Level	Beginner–Elementary
Time	10–20 minutes
Preparation	(Optionally) Objects, pictures or the names of items to be guessed written down

Procedure

1 Select an item to be guessed. This may be an actual object, a picture of one or just something you have thought up on the spur of the moment and written down.

2 Using only 'yes/no' questions, students try to guess what it is. For example:

A: Is it in the classroom?
B: No.
C: Can we eat it?
B: Yes.
D: Is it round?
B: Yes.
E: Is it an apple?
B: Yes.

3 The one who guesses the correct answer gets to choose the next item to be guessed.

Teaching tip

In any guessing game, it may happen that someone who has already been the 'knower' (of the thing to be guessed) guesses the right answer again. It is useful to have a standard rule that anyone who guesses the correct answer a second time gets to choose who shall be the next 'knower'. Thus the successful guesser is rewarded with the privilege of choosing, while more students get opportunities to be the 'knower'.

Notes

1 Beginners have a smaller vocabulary to choose from and therefore can go straight into the guessing process. More advanced learners need to have the range of possible answers narrowed, so give them a hint to start them off: for example, whether the item is animal, vegetable or mineral, what letter the word begins with or any random hint chosen by the 'knower'.

2 If the item to be guessed is a concrete noun, try to use a (hidden) actual object, or a toy representation of one, rather than just an image in your mind. The object can then be revealed when it is guessed. (Students, particularly – but not only – young or teenage ones, find it far more motivating to guess an actual object than just an abstract idea.) If you can't use actual objects, pictures are better than written or imagined definitions. The successful guesser can then get the object or the picture as a (temporary!) reward for guessing.

Variations

1 There are many variations on *Guessing*, with corresponding variation as to the level of vocabulary needed. For example:

guessing what I have in my bag ('Do you have …?')
guessing mimes ('Are you drinking?') (see *17.2.3 Guessing mimes*)
guessing occupations ('Do you work in a school?')
guessing where something is hidden ('Is it in this room?') (see *16.4 Guessing locations*)
guessing celebrities ('Are you a movie star?')
guessing verbs ('Can I do this?')
guessing famous events ('Did it happen in this century?')

2 The guessing activity can be made more brisk and motivating by the introduction of a limit on the number of questions that may be asked ('You have to guess the answer in not more than 20 questions') or on the time available ('You have 2 minutes to guess the answer').

Follow-up

1 Students do the same activity in groups of five or six, sitting round a table. Give each group a pile of cards with pictures or words to be guessed, face down in the centre of the table; each student in turn takes a card and challenges the others to guess it.

2 For homework, students write a series of four or five questions, together with the appropriate answers ('yes' or 'no', plus, possibly, short 'tag' answers), intended to lead to a certain solution. You, then, have not only to check the grammar of the questions, but also guess the solutions. For example, a student might write:

   Does it have four legs? No.
   Does it fly? No.
   Does it swim? Yes.
   Can we eat it? Yes.

   Similar sets of questions composed by students may be brought to class for students to exchange between themselves and guess each other's items; or both writing and reading may be done as a classroom activity.

> **Teaching tip**
>
> In any question-and-answer-based activity like guessing, most of the class should be questioning, and only one person (or possibly two) should be the 'knower' answering the questions. If it's done the other way round, the load on the guesser is too heavy, while most of the class have too little to do – with the result that the process slows down and becomes tedious, and the practice is inefficient.

7.1.2 Common denominator

Focus	'Yes/no' questions
Age	Any
Level	Beginner–Intermediate
Time	10–20 minutes

Procedure

1 Think of a certain feature that may be common to various objects, ('roundness', for example), and put one such object into a sentence. For example:

   I love the sun.

2 Students then try to find out what your 'common denominator' is by asking questions based on the original sentence. A student who thinks you are thinking of 'hot' might ask:

   Do you love fire?

   and one who thinks it is 'something in the sky' might ask:

   Do you love clouds?

   to both of which you answer 'no'. A question such as:

   Do you love oranges?

   however, since you are thinking of 'round', obviously gets the answer 'yes'.

3 The guessers only have one 'direct question' – for example:

   Is the answer 'round'?

   – so they have to be very sure that they are right before asking it – which means asking several verifying 'Do you love ...?' questions even after they are fairly sure they know the answer.

Variation

The original sentence does not, of course, have to begin 'I love ...' You can vary it according to the kind of verb, or tense, you want to practise in the interrogative. See *Box 7.1.2a* for some possible base sentences and *Box 7.1.2b* for some possible common denominators.

Box 7.1.2a Common denominator

Possible base sentences

- I / my friend love(s) ...
- We're going on a picnic tomorrow, and we'll take ...
- I'm reading a book about ...
- Yesterday Jeremy went for a walk, and he saw ...
- I'm going to buy ...
- In our house there is ...
- I would like to have ...

Box 7.1.2b: Common denominator

Possible common denominators

- round
- square
- soft
- hard
- long
- short
- red
- yellow
- green
- blue

- is smaller (or larger) than a person
- has a handle
- is in this classroom
- floats on water
- can fly
- can be eaten or drunk
- can be held in the hand
- is a machine
- breaks if it is dropped
- makes a noise
- is an animal product
- works on electricity
- contains five or more letters
- contains *t* (or any letter of your choice)
- begins with the same letter as the name of the guesser
- is made of metal (or wood, or any substance of your choice)

7.1.3 Questionnaires

Focus 'Yes/no' questions to elicit real information
Age Any
Level Elementary–Intermediate
Time 30–40 minutes
Preparation Copies of questionnaires (see *Boxes 7.1.3a* and *7.1.3b* for some examples)

Procedure

1 Present the questionnaire, and make sure everyone understands it. Decide together what to put at the head of the last column (a pastime or skill that is relevant to the students).

2 Students work in pairs, asking each other the questions and writing down the answers.

3 As each pair finishes, they separate and look for another partner with whom to repeat the process, until they have filled in at least two or three lines in their questionnaire forms.

Variations

1 Other questionnaires in this book that can be used similarly may be found in *Boxes 10.4a–c, 17.1.4* and *21.2.2a–f*.

2 Instead of the questionnaire being supplied ready-made, it may be designed by the students, working in pairs or groups. Provide them with some topics they may base their questions on. For example:

tastes in food and drink
sleeping habits
study habits
ideas on what an ideal husband/wife/partner should be like
opinions on a current local issue

The question forms used should be checked by you before the questionnaires are administered and filled in.

Follow-up

1 After filling in three lines or so of the questionnaire, students meet up in pairs and ask about someone else whom their new partner has already interviewed. So the questions will begin 'Does X ...?'
2 Later, discuss the findings with the class. What do most people in this class like doing? What kinds of skills do most people in this class have? Who knows how to ...?

Box 7.1.3a: Questionnaires

Answer code:	✓✓ = yes, a lot		✓= yes, but not a lot		✗ = no	
	Do you . . .					
Name:	... listen to music?	... do sports?	... read?	... go shopping?	... play computer games?	

Box 7.1.3b: Questionnaires

Answer code:	✓✓ = yes, quite well		✓= yes, but not very well			✗ = no
	Do you . . .					
Name:	... play a musical instrument?	... use a computer?	... swim?	... skate or ski?	... drive?	

7.1.4 Don't say yes or no

Focus Freely composed 'yes/no' questions
Age Any
Level Elementary–Intermediate
Time 10–20 minutes

Procedure

1 Explain that the aim is to get someone to say 'yes' or 'no'. Start by being the answerer yourself, invite students to ask you 'yes/no' questions and answer them with phrases like:

I agree.
He is.
We do.
Certainly.
Of course not.

When they manage to catch you out and you do say 'yes' or 'no' – proceed to step 2!

2 A student volunteer takes your place and tries to avoid 'yes' or 'no' in answer to questions from other students. You may also contribute questions. Add a couple of extra rules at this point: you can't give the same answer twice; and a pause of longer than five seconds is unacceptable.
3 If, however, 'yes' or 'no' is said, or if the answerer takes more than five seconds to answer, he/she is 'out', and another volunteer takes his/her place.

Notes

1 With less advanced or smaller classes, it can be helpful to think of a variety of appropriate 'yes/no' questions in advance and write them on the board so that students have a ready-made selection to choose from.
2 You may also need to review all sorts of useful 'tag' answers like 'We are', 'I would', etc., as well as adverbs that can substitute for positive/negative answers, for example: *of course/not, sure, absolutely, probably, possibly, definitely, always, never, not likely, not at all, impossible.*

Variations

1 An answerer who survives more than two minutes is declared a champion, is congratulated and steps down in glory! (Otherwise some turns can go on too long, and other students don't get a chance to try answering.)
2 The activity can be done in groups, but then the groups need to be fairly big (at least six students).

7.2 'WH-' QUESTIONS

7.2.1 Find someone with the answer

Focus Reading 'Wh-' questions and their answers
Age Any
Level Elementary–Intermediate
Time 5–10 minutes
Preparation Slips of paper with simple 'Wh-' questions on them; separate slips with corresponding answers. In total, there should be rather more slips than there are students in the class. For example, for a class of 20 students, you should have about 15 questions and 15 corresponding answers (see *Boxes 7.2.1a*, *7.2.1b* and *7.2.1c* for some examples).

Procedure

1 Each student gets one question slip or one answer slip, distributed at random. You will be left with a random set of questions and answers in reserve.
2 Students walk round the classroom, reading out their slips to each other, and try to find matching questions and answers.
3 Pairs who find a match come to you and get new slips from your reserve.
4 This goes on until you have none left and everyone has found at least one matching slip.

Teaching tip

Keep these slips for re-use later: they are a good way to divide the class into random pairs in preparation for pair work.

Box 7.2.1a: Find someone with the answer

Questions

What language do they speak in Brazil?	What colour is the sky?
What language do they speak in Australia?	Where is Montreal?
What language do they speak in Quebec?	Where is Geneva?
What is the capital of China?	Where is Teheran?
Which country's flag is green with a red circle in its centre?	What colour is a panda?
Which continent has the most people?	What colour is a lemon?
What is the first month of the year?	What is three times six?
How many tens are there in a hundred?	Who was the Roman who gave his name to the month of July?

Box 7.2.1b: Find someone with the answer

Questions

How many grams are there in a kilo?	Who wrote *Winnie the Pooh*?
When did the first man walk on the moon?	Who wrote *Macbeth*?
How many legs does a spider have?	What is seven plus eight?
How many legs does a horse have?	Where did Cleopatra live?
How many days are there in a week?	How many days are there in June?
What is cheese made from?	What is bread made from?
Which came first, the Bronze Age or the Iron Age?	Who invented the telephone?
In which country is Dubai?	Which country does the island of Tasmania belong to?

Box 7.2.1c: Find someone with the answer

Answers

Portuguese	English	French	Beijing
Bangladesh	Asia	January	ten
a thousand	1969	eight	four
seven	milk	the Bronze Age	blue
in Canada	in Switzerland	in Iran	black and white
yellow	eighteen	Julius Caesar	A. A. Milne
William Shakespeare	fifteen	in Egypt	thirty
flour	Alexander Graham Bell	the United Arab Emirates	Australia

Answers (Boxes 7.2.1a and 7.2.1b)

What language do they speak in Brazil? (Portuguese)
What colour is the sky? (blue)
What language do they speak in Australia? (English)
Where is Montreal? (in Canada)
What language do they speak in Quebec? (French)
Where is Geneva? (in Switzerland)
What is the capital of China? (Beijing)
Where is Teheran? (in Iran)
Which country's flag is green with a red circle in its centre? (Bangladesh)
What colour is a panda? (black and white)
Which continent has the most people? (Asia)
What colour is a lemon? (yellow)
What is the first month of the year? (January)
What is three times six? (eighteen)
How many tens are there in a hundred? (ten)
Who was the Roman who gave his name to the month of July? (Julius Caesar)
How many grams are there in a kilo? (a thousand)
Who wrote Winnie the Pooh? (A.A. Milne)

Answers (Boxes 7.2.1a and 7.2.1b)

When did the first man walk on the moon? (1969)
Who wrote Macbeth? (William Shakespeare)
How many legs does a spider have? (eight)
What is seven plus eight? (fifteen)
How many legs does a horse have? (four)
Where did Cleopatra live? (in Egypt)
How many days are there in a week? (seven)
How many days are there in June? (thirty)
What is cheese made from? (milk)
What is bread made from? (flour)
Which came first, the Bronze Age or the Iron Age? (the Bronze Age)
Who invented the telephone? (Alexander Graham Bell)
In which country is Dubai? (the United Arab Emirates)
Which country does the island of Tasmania belong to? (Australia)

7.2.2 Quizzes

Focus	Reading and answering 'Wh-' questions (Variation: composing 'Wh-' questions)
Age	Teenager–Adult
Level	Elementary–Intermediate
Time	20–30 minutes
Preparation	Copies of a quiz (see *Box 7.2.2* for an example)

Procedure

1 Tell the class you want to find out how much general knowledge they have. They should work in pairs or small groups, trying to fill in the answers to the quiz.

2 Then they read out questions and check answers. How did the class, as a whole, do?

Follow-up

Without looking at the original quiz, how many of the questions (and their correct answers) can they recall later in the lesson – or the following day?

Variations

1 Put students in pairs or small groups, and give them ten minutes to compose as many general-knowledge questions as they can. Each pair/group then asks the class their questions.

2 The class can be divided into two teams and compete against each other: who can answer the most questions from a given quiz?

3 Suggest they compose a similar quiz for you, the teacher, on a local topic on which they are experts and you, possibly, are not.

Box 7.2.2: Quizzes

General knowledge quiz

1 Where is Toronto?

2 Who spoke Latin?

3 What's the formula for finding out the area of a circle?

4 Which is the longest river in Asia?

5 How many players are there in a football team?

6 What is the capital of India?

7 Who was Elvis Presley?

8 What was Sherlock Holmes' occupation?

9 When did the Second World War start?

10 Which country was *The Lord of the Rings* filmed in?

11 How do elephants sleep – standing up or lying down?

12 What are the five senses?

13 What kind of an animal is a dingo?

14 What is a gondola?

15 What is the capital of Ethiopia?

16 What is the official language of Iran?

17 How many states are there in the USA?

18 How often are the Olympic Games held?

19 In which country is Johannesburg?

20 What happened to Pompeii?

Teaching tip

When giving a task to compose text of any kind, it's a good idea to provide a time limit rather than a limit of text: 'Do as much as you can in ten minutes' rather than 'Write ten questions'. This allows each student/pair to work at their own speed and level, and avoids the situation where faster workers finish too early and/or slower ones don't have enough time.

Answers (Box 7.2.2)

1 in Canada	11 standing up
2 the Romans	12 sight, hearing, touch, smell, taste
3 πr^2	13 a wild dog
4 the Yangtze	14 a boat (in Venice)
5 11	15 Addis Ababa
6 New Delhi	16 Persian
7 a pop singer	17 50
8 detective	18 every 4 years
9 1939	19 South Africa
10 New Zealand	20 It was destroyed by a volcano.

7.2.3 Your own comprehension questions

Focus	Composing 'Wh-' questions
Age	Any
Level	Elementary–Intermediate
Time	20–30 minutes

Procedure

1 Provide a reading text – preferably one you are working on anyway in your textbook.

2 Invite students to write their own comprehension questions for it. They may work individually or in pairs. Give them ten minutes to compose as many as they can.

3 Students read out their questions and challenge you to answer them. You are not allowed to look at the text (but you can, of course, correct the grammar of their questions!).

Variations

1 If the text has conventional comprehension questions following it, an easier variation is to ask students to select only some of them and say why they think these are the most important.

2 Invite students to write comprehension questions for a non-existent text: ('Why did Mr Perkins put marmalade on the cat?'). They then exchange their sets of questions and try to compose a text on which the questions might have been asked.

7.2.4 Paired cloze

Focus	'Wh-' questions to ascertain missing information
Age	Teenager–Adult
Level	Intermediate–Advanced
Time	30–40 minutes
Preparation	Copies of two versions of the same text, each with different factual items missing (times, places, distances, etc.) (see *Boxes 7.2.4a* and *7.2.4b* for examples)

Procedure

1 Students work in pairs. Each partner has a different version of the same text (*Version A* or *Version B*).

2 Students have to find out the information in order to fill in the missing items in their texts, but the rules are:
   a. They may not read out gapped sentences from their own text.
   b. They may only ask 'Wh-' questions in order to elicit the necessary information from their partner.

Notes

1 The text provided here is quite long and takes a while to complete. Tell the students that the last paragraph is optional: if they've filled in all the gaps in the earlier sections, that's fine.

2 When designing your own 'paired cloze' texts, choose a text that has plenty of factual information in it. You may find that you need to clarify the information required to fill a gap with a hint (e.g. [year], as I have done here), otherwise it's not always clear what kind of information is required.

Teaching tip

When doing any task based on a text or set number of items, it is a good strategy to define the last part of the text or the last few items as 'optional' only. Then slower students don't have to feel they have in some way failed if they complete the 'core' task without the optional extra. This also helps to solve the problem of students who finish the core exercise early, are bored and need further challenge.

Box 7.2.4a: Paired cloze

Version A

Exploring new places is exciting and challenging, but it can also be extremely dangerous. It can even result in death.

The American pilot, ____________ [first name] Earhart, for example, disappeared in 1937. Earhart was trying to fly around the world from west to east. She took off from ______________ [place], California, in a two-seater plane, and flew across the South Atlantic, Africa, Arabia and ____________________ [area]. After arriving in New Guinea, she set off for an island in the mid-Pacific nearly 4,100 km away, and was never seen or heard of again.

Another disappearance happened in the Himalayas of ________________ [country] in 1924. Two British climbers, _____________ [first name] Mallory and Andrew Irvine, reached a point about ________ [number] metres from the top of Mount Everest, the highest mountain in the world, and then disappeared. Other climbers reached the top of Everest in 1953, but no trace was ever found of Mallory and Irvine[1].

There were also disappearances in the 19th century. For example, in 1845, two British ships, the ____________ [name] and the ___________ [name], left England to explore the area north of Canada. The ships, which had a total crew of ______ [number] men, were commanded by Sir John Franklin, one of the most famous explorers of the time. They were last seen by another ship near the coast of ______________ [country], and then they vanished. In 1851, two ships were seen on a huge floating island of ice. Then, in _______ [year], a search party found a message under some stones on an island north of Canada. It said that ____________________ [people] might still be alive.

[1] Since this text was written, George Mallory's body has been found.

Jack Baum and Michael Toben
Practice Your Unseens 3

Box 7.2.4b: Paired cloze

Version B

Exploring new places is exciting and challenging, but it can also be extremely dangerous. It can even result in death.

The American pilot, Amelia Earhart, for example, disappeared in _____ [year]. Earhart was trying to fly around the world from west to east. She took off from Oakland, California, in a two-seater plane, and flew across the ________________ [ocean], Africa, Arabia and south-east Asia. After arriving in New Guinea, she set off for an island in the mid-Pacific nearly _______ [number] km away, and was never seen or heard of again.

Another disappearance happened in the Himalayas of Nepal in ________ [year]. Two British climbers, George Mallory and __________ [first name] Irvine, reached a point about 300 metres from the top of Mount Everest, the highest mountain in the world, and then disappeared. Other climbers reached the top of Everest in _________ [year], but no trace was ever found of Mallory and Irvine[1].

There were also disappearances in the 19th century. For example, in 1845, two British ships, the *Erebus* and the *Terror*, left ___________ [place] to explore the area ___________ [location]. The ships, which had a total crew of 120 men, were commanded by ____________________ [name], one of the most famous explorers of the time. They were last seen by another ship near the coast of Greenland, and then they vanished. In 1851, ____________ [things] were seen on a huge floating island of ice. Then, in 1857, a search party found a message under ________________ [things] on an island north of Canada. It said that 105 of the men might still be alive.

[1] Since this text was written, George Mallory's body has been found.

Jack Baum and Michael Toben
Practice Your Unseens 3

7.3 ALL TYPES OF QUESTIONS

7.3.1 Dialogues

Focus	All types of questions, within dialogues
Age	Young–Teenager
Level	Beginner–Intermediate
Time	5–10 minutes, several times in different lessons
Preparation	Short conversations between two speakers involving questions (see *Box 7.3.1* for some examples)

Procedure

1 Present the dialogue orally – with or without a written version on the board – and get the students to learn it by heart.

2 Students then perform it. This can be done by a single pair of students in front of the class or by all the students, in pairs, simultaneously. In either case it should be performed as dramatically as possible.

3 The dialogue is reviewed and performed again in later lessons. Tell students to vary it: in tempo, volume or tone ('Do the dialogue fast/slowly ... loudly/softly ... in a high/low voice ...'); or in mood ('Do the dialogue angrily ... sadly ... laughingly ... dramatically ... fearfully ...').

Follow-up

1 Ask students what they think the context might be. What's the situation? Who are the characters? What has just happened? Each dialogue, of course, is open to multiple interpretations.

2 Invite students to suggest variations: to change the words in order to make new situations. Further exchanges can be added to develop the situation in different ways.

Note

If you have taught students rules about how to form the interrogative, draw their attention to the form of the questions they are using in the dialogues and how these conform to the rules.

Box 7.3.1: Dialogues

Dialogue 1

A: What are you doing?
B: I'm going outside.
A: Why? (*pause*) Why are you going outside?
B: None of your business.

Dialogue 2

A: What do you have in your hand?
B: This? It's a frog.
A: Are you sure?
B: Yes, of course I'm sure.
A: Amazing!

Dialogue 3

A: Did you remember to call him?
B: No, I didn't … Oh no! What shall I do?
A: Can you call him now?
B: Too late! Disaster!

Dialogue 4

A: Are you all right?
B: Yes, I'm fine.
A: Don't you want to come inside?
B: No, I'm quite happy where I am, thank you.

Dialogue 5

A: Hi … can you help me?
B: What's the problem?
A: Well, it's rather difficult to explain …
B: Why don't you sit down?

7.3.2 Wrangling

Focus	Oral question forms
Age	Young–Teenager
Level	Beginner–Elementary
Time	5–10 minutes

Procedure

1 Choose a single exchange from a dialogue (see *Box 7.3.1* for some examples).
2 Invite two volunteer students to perform it.
3 They continue to repeat the exchange, as assertively as they can, each trying to wear the other down. The first to give up or laugh is the loser.

7.3.3 Beat the clock

Focus	Simple questions and answers
Age	Young
Level	Beginner–Elementary
Time	5–10 minutes

Procedure

1 Choose a simple interactive exchange like

What's your name?
My name's ...

or:

How are you?
I'm fine, thank you.

(or see *Box 7.3.3* for some more examples).
2 Look at your watch and say 'Go'. Student A asks Student B the question and is answered; Student B then turns to Student C and does the same ... and so on. A set order has to be organized in advance (round the circle, for example, if students are sitting in a circle). When they have finished, check your watch again, and see how long they took.
3 Repeat the process, challenging the class to beat their previous (time) record.

Note

If the class is very big, you may have to do the process with only part of the class, or divide them into two or more equal groups and let them compete: who can complete the chain faster?

Box 7.3.3: Beat the clock

Dialogue 1
What's the time?
It's six o'clock.

Dialogue 2
Where's my book?
I don't know.

Dialogue 3
What's the matter?
Nothing's the matter.

Dialogue 4
What do you think?
I've no idea!

Dialogue 5
What's the weather like?
It's sunny!

Dialogue 6
How's your family?
They're fine, thank you.

7.3.4 Answer with a question

Focus	Oral question forms
Age	Teenager–Adult
Level	Elementary–Intermediate
Time	10–20 minutes

Procedure

1 Two volunteer students stand before the class.
2 One asks the other any question they like. The other has to respond with a further question. The first student responds with a further question … and so on. They are not allowed to repeat a question that has already been asked. For example:

What's your name?
Why do you want to know?
Is the reason important?
What do you mean by 'important'?

Don't you know what it means?
Why should I?...

3 If they manage to complete three such exchanges (six questions), they have succeeded, and two other students take their place and try again. It's more difficult than it sounds!

7.3.5 Filling in forms

Focus	Asking questions and filling in brief answers
Age	Any
Level	Beginner–Elementary
Time	15–25 minutes
Preparation	Copies of simple forms (see *Boxes 7.3.5a Personal details* (for a form for adult learners) *7.3.5b Personal details* (for a form for younger learners) and *7.3.5c Personal profile*)

Procedure

1 Distribute copies of the appropriate form to students (form **a** for adults, **b** for younger learners or **c** for either age group). Make sure all the items are understood.

2 Tell them to work in pairs and interview each other in order to fill in the forms. All such information must be given only in response to a proper question: thus, given the cue 'Age', the asker must say 'How old are you?'.

3 During the process of supplying the information, the answerers may help or correct the askers in their questioning. Before giving in the filled-in forms, each student should check that his or her partner has in fact filled in the information correctly.

Variations

1 Each answerer has to give two false pieces of information in response to the questions asked; at the end, each student tries to identify his or her partner's lies. (This variation is, obviously, only feasible if the students know each other fairly well – and is one way of getting to know each other even better!)

2 Later, students may role play a different person: a celebrity, a fictional character or a locally known personality – and answer the questions in their 'new' persona.

Note

Some groups of students may feel it an intrusion on their privacy to provide details of age, telephone numbers and so on; in such cases use the third questionnaire rather than the first two.

Box 7.3.5a: Filling in forms

Personal details

Family name: ....

First name(s): ....

Date of birth: .... Place of birth: ....

Married/unmarried: ....

Children (if any): ....

Names and ages: ....

Occupation: ....

Nationality: ....

Home address: ....

....

Home telephone number: ....

Mobile number: ....

Email address: ....

Interests: ....

....

Box 7.3.5b: Filling in forms

Personal details

Family name: ....

First name(s): ....

Age: .... Place of birth: ....

Home address: ....

....

Telephone number: ....

Interests: ....

....

Box 7.3.5c: Filling in forms

Personal profile

Family name: ....

First name(s): ....

Occupation: ....

Home town: ....

Language(s): ....

Favourite colour: ....

Favourite leisure activity: ....

Favourite television programme: ....

Favourite famous person: ....

7.3.6 Preparing interviews

Focus	Writing and saying all sorts of questions to elicit information
Age	Any
Level	Elementary–Intermediate
Time	30–40 minutes

Procedure

1 Tell students they are to interview you for a television chat show and have to prepare a set of 10 to 20 questions to elicit information they want.

2 Give them 10 or 15 minutes to do so, working individually or in pairs. Help them with new vocabulary where necessary. You may wish them to write out the questions in full or just jot them down in brief note form.

3 They then interview you.

Variations

1 Invite a visitor to come to your class and be interviewed. Tell the students something about him/her, and have them prepare the questions ahead of time.

2 Role play yourself, or invite a student to role play, a celebrity or fictional character or someone with an unusual characteristic (see *Box 7.3.6*). Again, tell the students in advance who they are going to interview, and have them prepare questions as in *Procedure* above.

Box 7.3.6: Preparing interviews

People you could interview (as a role play):
Well-known personalities in politics, current affairs, entertainment, sports, the arts, broadcasting
Local people: other teachers or students from the school, well-known personalities from the community
People who have something unusual about them: a mother of 20 children; a professional stunt man/woman; the possessor of a pet elephant; a woman with 3 husbands; a man with 3 wives; a person 2.1 metres tall; a multimillionaire; someone who lives in a cave; an astronaut

7.3.7 Long subjects

Focus	Questions with long subjects
Age	Teenager–Adult
Level	Intermediate
Time	20–25 minutes

Procedure

1 Write at the top of the board:
When is Terry leaving?

2 Tell the students that they can add one, two or three more words to the subject ('Terry'): what do they suggest? They might suggest 'and his friend': you add these words to the sentence, keeping 'leaving' at the end and altering *is* to *are*:
When are Terry and his friend leaving?

3 Invite them to carry on adding two or three times more, until they have a ridiculously long subject – but the sentence still has to make sense!
When are Terry and his very nice friend from Berlin leaving?

4 Draw students' attention to the fact that even though it's a very long subject, the subject still comes before the main verb, not after it.

5 Now delete 'When are' and 'leaving', so that only the long subject remains on the board.

6 Do this again with four more sentences (see *Box 7.3.7* for some examples). By the end, you will be left with five long subjects on the board.

7 Challenge the students – possibly in a following lesson, or for homework – to reconstruct the question correctly for each subject.

Box 7.3.7: Long subjects

- When is Terry leaving?
- Are the boys listening to that music?
- What are those people saying?
- What do the students enjoy?
- Is the President staying here?

8 *Is/are* and *there is / there are*

8.1 Describing pictures

Focus	*Is/are* or *there is / there are* to describe a scene
Age	Young
Level	Beginner–Elementary
Time	10–15 minutes
Preparation	A big picture with plenty of clearly shown details displayed on the board (see *Boxes 8.1a*, *8.1b* and *8.1c* for some examples)

Procedure

1 Challenge the students to say at least 20 sentences about the picture within 2 minutes, using *(there) is* or *(there) are*. Write a tick on the board for every (correct) sentence they say, then count them up when the 2 minutes are finished.

2 If they managed it, show another picture and raise the objective to a higher number of sentences – however many you feel is a feasible goal.

Variations

1 Do the same in small groups. Give each group a picture, and tell them to choose one 'secretary' who writes the ticks. Wait until the second hand of your watch reaches 12, then say, 'Go!'. Stop them talking after exactly 2 minutes, and tell them to count up how many ticks they have. Then tell them to look at another picture and do it again, trying to break their previous record (they usually do).

2 Display two pictures of roughly similar subjects – but by no means identical – and ask students to suggest differences. For example:

The horse in Picture B is white, but the horse in Picture A is black.

3 Show the picture, and then hide it and challenge students to recall what is in it, using *is/are* or *there is / there are.*

4 Ask the students to do the same in writing; give them 15 minutes.

Teaching tip

A time limit adds a lot to the 'game-like' feeling of an activity, and can be used with many tasks. Look at your watch very obviously, don't let the class start speaking until you say 'Go!' and stop them dramatically when the time is up.

Box 8.1a: Describing pictures

Box 8.1b: Describing pictures

Box 8.1c: Describing pictures

8.2 Picture dictation

Focus	*Is/are* or *there is / there are* to describe a scene
Age	Young
Level	Beginner–Elementary
Time	15–20 minutes

Procedure

Draw a large rectangular frame on the board, and invite students to tell you what to draw in it. You might start by suggesting it is a room, then saying, 'There's a table in the room,' and drawing it in the centre of the space as a first cue. Students suggest further details. For example:

> There's a vase on the table.
> The vase is blue.

Variations

1 You may, of course, invite students to do the drawing, but this, in my experience, tends to slow things down somewhat; better to do the sketching yourself, even if it is very unartistic, and gain more time for language practice. An alternative is to use prepared cut-out drawings: cut-out paper ones for a white- or blackboard, a prepared set of clip art items for an interactive whiteboard or PowerPoint presentation. In either case, these are shown to the students at the side of the board in advance. This, of course, both guides and limits the kinds of contribution available to the students.

2 Use other first-cue bases for a picture dictation. For example: a tree, a road, a stick figure, a house, a line of distant mountains.

3 The exercise can be made more interesting by asking students to describe not just a conventional scene, but an unusual one: an extremely untidy room, for example, or their ideal classroom, or an outdoor scene on an imaginary alien planet.

4 Put students into pairs, and tell one to dictate a picture to the other. Then they switch.

8.3 Find a twin picture

Focus	*Is/are* in questions and answers
Age	Young
Level	Beginner–Elementary
Time	10–15 minutes
Preparation	A set of pictures (see *Boxes 8.3a* and *8.3b*); make two copies of each picture. The total number of pictures should be slightly more than the number of students in the class: so if, for example, you have a class of 20, you only need to make double copies of 13–14 different pictures.

Procedure

1 Give each student one picture, which they are not allowed to show each other. Each student then has to find someone who has the exact duplicate of his or her picture: they do this by asking questions. For example:

Is the cat black?
Where is the dog?

2 Students who have found twins bring them to you; you check they are right, and give them further pictures from the reserve until all are gone.

3 The activity ends when all the pictures are paired.

Variations

1 The activity can be made slightly longer if there are three copies of each picture. Each student then has to find two others with the same picture.

2 To increase the challenge, use the colour version of the pictures from CD-ROM *Box 8.3c*.

3 Put students into pairs, and give each partner a picture (make sure these are not 'twins'). Without looking at each other's pictures, they have to find the differences between them, asking and answering in English. When they have finished, they look at the pictures, check they were right and bring them back to you to get another pair.

Teaching tip

Teachers are sometimes worried that in an activity not under direct teacher supervision, as here, the students will start over-using L1. Not that L1 use is always bad! – but it can sometimes increase to the point at which students are getting very little practice in the target language. In my experience, this happens mainly when the vocabulary needed is too difficult: either it's not known at all or requires too much of an effort to retrieve. So in pair/group work activities, keep the vocabulary very simple (as it is in this one): that way, students will find it easy to keep to the target language.

Box 8.3a: Find a twin picture

Box 8.3b: Find a twin picture

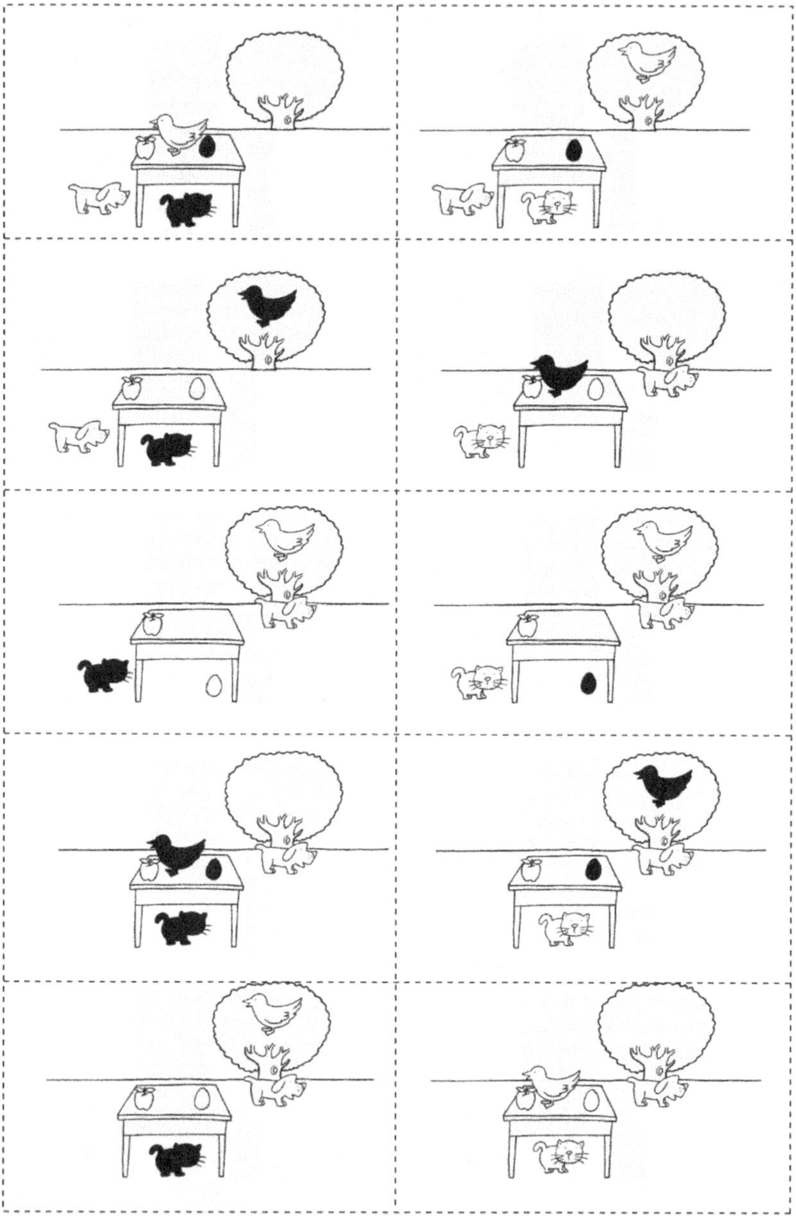

8.4 Reverse guessing (1)

Focus	Affirmative and negative sentences with pronouns and *is/are*
Age	Any
Level	Beginner–Elementary
Time	15–20 minutes

Procedure

1 Choose a person or animal or thing that all the class knows in English. Tell or show all the class but one what it is.

2 The student who does not know what it is stands in front of the class.

3 Tell the other students to volunteer hints in the form of positive and negative statements. For example:

It isn't in the classroom.
She is tall and thin.
He has black hair.

Notes

1 Verbs other than *is/are* may well come up, as in the third example above: this is fine. Most of the sentences are very likely to use *is/are* or *isn't/aren't*.

2 Don't be tempted to do this the other way round (one 'hinter', all the class 'guessers'); the result is that only one student gets the active practice, and the process is a lot slower (see *Teaching tip*, p. 93).

8.5 Is it in my bag?

Focus	Affirmative and negative sentences with nouns and *is/are, there is / there are*
Age	Young
Level	Beginner
Time	10–15 minutes
Preparation	A set of 8 items that the students know how to say in English, pictured or real, in a bag. These should include representations of items that are unlikely really to be in a bag: e.g. a tractor (represented by a toy), a baby (represented by a doll); but also things that might be real, e.g. a book.

Procedure

1 Write up on the board a list of 12 items, including the 8 you have in your bag.

2 Tell the students that of these items, 8 are in fact in your bag, and 4 are not.

3 Ask them to guess which of the items they think are in your bag and which are not. For example:

   The tractor isn't in your bag.
   The book is in your bag.

4 Add a ✓ or a ✗ by each item to indicate what they thought.

5 Then take the items out of your bag one by one, saying, for example:

   There *is* a tractor in my bag! You're wrong!
   There *is* a book in my bag! You're right!

6 Comment on their score!

Notes

1 The second time you do this, of course, the students know that there are going to be some unlikely items; but it's still fun to try to guess which items are in the bag and which are not, and have the actual items revealed at the end.

2 If you want to focus on *there is / there are* throughout, you can ask for students' initial responses in the form 'There is a book in your bag', etc.

9 Modals

9.1 Guessing by abilities

Focus	*Can/can't* to describe abilities or possibilities
Age	Any
Level	Elementary–Intermediate
Time	10–20 minutes

Procedure

1. Choose the name of an object, an animal or a person well known to the class. Tell all the class but one what it is.
2. The student who does not know stands in front of the class.
3. The rest of the class give him or her hints based on what the item *can* or *can't* do (mainly animals or people), or what we *can* or *can't* do with it (mainly objects). For example, if the item is a koala they might say:

   It can climb trees.
   It can carry its baby.
   You can't buy one in a shop.

   If it is an egg, they might say:

   You can break it.
   You can use it to make a cake.
4. The student has to guess what the item is.
5. The guesser may also ask *can/can't* questions but may not guess what the subject actually is, even if they think they know, until the other students have given all their hints.

Follow-up

For homework, students choose a subject of their own to describe in the same way in writing for you to guess – or for other students to guess in the following lesson.

9.2 Uses of an object

Focus	*Can/could* to describe possibilities
Age	Any
Level	Elementary–Intermediate
Time	15–30 minutes
Preparation	A picture of a simple object, or (better) the object itself (see *Box 9.2* for some examples)

Procedure

1 Invite the students to suggest as many original uses for the object as they can, using *can* or *could* (whichever you want to practise). For example, if the object is a pen, students might suggest:

You can use it to dig holes.
You could scratch your head with it.

2 After initial demonstration with the full class, divide the students into groups, and give each group an object. They have three or four minutes to think up all the uses they can, noted by a 'secretary'. Help them with new vocabulary as necessary.

3 The groups report back their suggestions, which are usually entertaining enough in themselves to provide interest; or, if all the groups have the same object, the activity can be made into a competition between groups to see who can produce the most, or the most original, ideas.

Note

With beginner classes, limited usually to the modal *can* in this activity, you can widen the range of possible sentences by saying that anything at all you can do with the object is acceptable, it doesn't have to be an actual use. For example:

You can hold it.
You can put it on the table.

With more advanced classes, however, I find it better to set the rule that the sentences must express an actual, feasible (though not necessarily likely!) use of the object (as in the examples in *Procedure* above): this is more of a challenge and produces more varied, interesting contributions.

Box 9.2: Uses of an object

a cup	a box of matches
a stone	a nail file
a bucket	a lump of clay
a screwdriver	a hat
a piece of string	a belt
a sheet	a coin

9.3 Desert island equipment

Focus *Can/could/might* to express possibilities
Age Any
Level Intermediate–Advanced
Time 30–40 minutes
Preparation A set of ten small pictures of objects for each group (see *Box 9.3*)

Procedure

1 Tell the students they are stranded on a desert island. They have a set of items saved from the shipwreck, for which they need to find uses.
2 Suggest, for example, 'a tablecloth', and ask them what use they can suggest for it. They might say:
We could use the tablecloth as a flag to signal to ships.
or:
Someone might wear a tablecloth as a dress if they lost their clothes in the shipwreck.
3 Put the students into groups, and challenge them to find uses for all ten objects. They can also think of uses that combine different objects.
4 When the first group finishes, stop everyone.
5 Share the ideas the different groups had for the different items.

Variation

The activity may be presented as a competition between students or between groups: who can find the most, or the most interesting and original, uses?

Box 9.3: Desert island equipment

A TELEPHONE BOOK

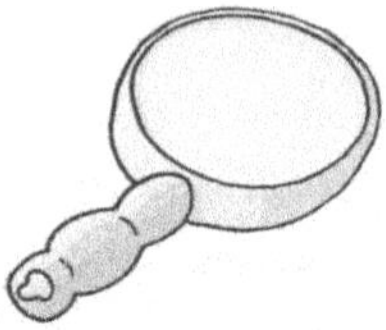

A MAGNIFYING GLASS

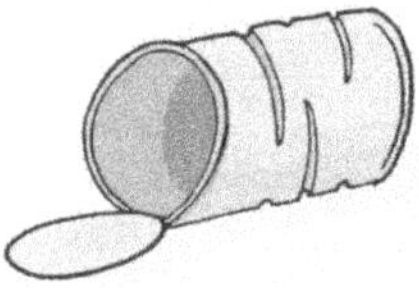

AN EMPTY TIN CAN

A TRUMPET

A BALL OF STRING

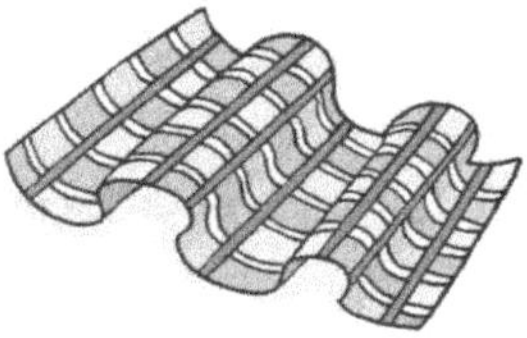

A BLANKET

A WOODEN SPOON

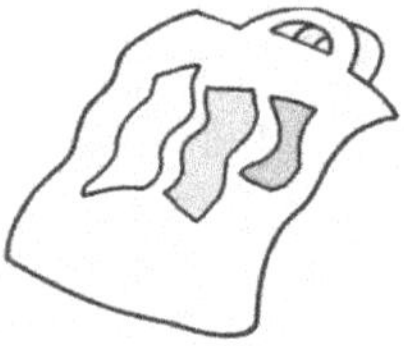

A PLASTIC BAG

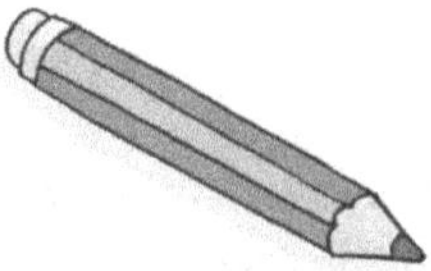

A PENCIL

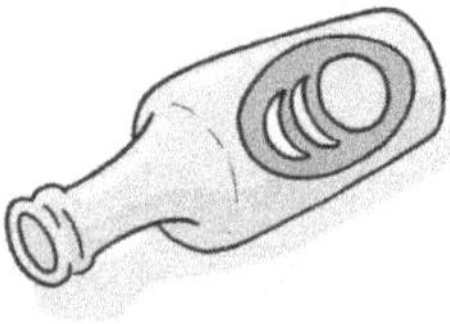

A BOTTLE

9.4 Games and their rules

Focus	*Must* / *have to* / *mustn't* / *can't* to express obligation or prohibition
Age	Any
Level	Elementary–Intermediate
Time	10–20 minutes

Procedure

1 Choose a game that the students all know. Write up on the board some basic facts about it: the objective, number of players, equipment, amount of time and space needed. Give some basic vocabulary essential to a description of the game.

2 Then invite students to list the game's rules, using modals such as *must*, *have to*, *mustn't*, *can't*. They may write down rules and later read them out or go straight into oral suggestions.

Variations

1 Divide students into groups, and give each group a different well-known game; ask them to write down (as a group) as many rules as they can think of in ten minutes on a sheet of paper. They then exchange papers, and correct and add to each other's lists. And so on, until all groups have seen all papers. When you have checked the results, these may be copied out and displayed.

2 If you have a class of students from various different cultures, then each can write about rules of games from home that they think other students may not be familiar with; then describe them to each other.

3 Ask groups to make up a new game. Perhaps provide them with a name for a game to start them off (see *Box 9.4* for some examples).

Box 9.4: Games and their rules

Hand-balloon	Reverse-race	Break the pot
Ice-skate drawing	Water-tennis	Nose hockey
Cycle-ball	Classroom handball	Bubble contest

Language tip

Either *can't* or *mustn't* can be used to express a prohibition: but *can't* is more common and natural in most contexts.

9.5 Rules and recommendations

Focus	*Must / mustn't / can't / have to / should / shouldn't* to express rules or recommendations
Age	Any
Level	Intermediate–Advanced
Time	20–25 minutes

Procedure

1 Ask students to write down any rules and recommendations which they think a new teacher coming to teach at this school, or on this course, should know. Rules should be phrased with *must* or *have to / mustn't* or *can't*, recommendations with *should/shouldn't*. For example:

You must come to lessons on time.
You mustn't use your mobile phone during lessons.
You shouldn't give very much homework!

2 Help individuals with new vocabulary as needed. Then hear their suggestions, and perhaps list them on the board.

Variations

1 Do the same for rules for a new student.

2 Ask each student to think of a job they know a lot about (perhaps their own or that of a near relative). Each student writes on the board their name together with the name of the occupation. From the list on the board, each student then chooses an occupation they don't know very much about, and makes up some questions to ask about it (which can use other modals as well, such as *can*). For example:

Do you have to ...?
Can you ...?

Individuals then ask their questions, in the full class, and the 'experts' suggest answers.

3 Instead of an occupation, give the students a place or situation which carries its own rules and recommendations: the reading room of a library, for example; a nature reserve; a museum; a train or bus.

Follow-up

Decide with the class which are the three most important rules and the three most important recommendations of those they thought of.

> **Language tip**
>
> You might like to make your more advanced students aware that *have to* is more natural than *must* in talking about a rule that is already fixed; *must* is more likely to be used when the rule is being imposed by the speaker (or negotiated between speaker and hearer).

9.6 Duties and privileges

Focus	*Can / may / can't / must / mustn't / don't have to* to define duties or privileges
Age	Teenager–Adult
Level	Intermediate–Advanced
Time	30–40 minutes

Procedure

1 Tell the class to imagine that they are responsible for finding a suitable candidate to fill a position they know something about: a new teacher or student, a school secretary, a security guard, for example. They have to write out an informal job description which might serve as a basis for interview. What duties, obligations or privileges might they mention? They can also mention negative ones (*don't have to ...*).

2 Students write their suggestions down. For example:

    You must be on duty at least seven hours a day.
    You can/may have a company car.
    You don't have to be a man!

3 They may do this individually or in small groups, pooling their ideas later.

4 The resulting description may be written up and displayed, and/or furnish a basis for a general discussion.

Variations

1 You might suggest that students add also some qualifications or personality characteristics that the candidate should/must/mustn't have. For example:

    You must have a driving licence.
    You should have a warm and outgoing personality.

2 For homework, students write about the duties and privileges of a job they are familiar with: what they do themselves as an occupation, or what their parents or other members of the family do.

9.7 Modal symbols

Focus	*Can / can't / must / mustn't / have to / may* to express permission, possibilities, obligation or prohibition
Age	Any
Level	Intermediate–Advanced
Time	25–30 minutes
Preparation	Well-known symbols (see *Box 5.5*) shown on the board or copied for students; for step 2, copies of the abstract symbols (see *Box 9.7*)

Procedure

1 Using the more well-known symbols (*Box 5.5*), ask the students to tell you what each means, using *can, can't, must, have to* or *mustn't*. Check the correct interpretation of each symbol (see *Meanings* (*Box 5.5*)).

2 Distribute the table of less well-known symbols (*Box 9.7*), and ask students to tell you what they think their significance is. They can suggest more than one interpretation for each item; but they all have to be expressed using the appropriate modals. The students may relate to the items in any order they like.

3 If you feel it is appropriate, reveal the actual meanings (*Original meanings* (*Box 9.7*) on p. 136). (Note that students are not expected to guess these, so they are not expressed as modal sentences.

Variation

Ask the class to suggest warnings, suggestions, etc. that could be posted at different places in the school and to devise symbols for them.

> **Teaching tip**
>
> Unless the items in a list are in some kind of logical sequence (a narrative, for example), there's no need to go through them in sequential order (number one first, then number two, then number three ...). Invite students to choose any one they like and relate to it; then any other they like ... and so on. Eventually you finish them all: but the opportunity to choose enables students to relax and choose their own favourites to relate to earlier. It also results in a slightly faster pace overall.

Box 9.7: Modal symbols

Meanings (Box 5.5)

1 You must / have to stop.
2 You can't/mustn't drink the water.
3 You can/may wash your hands here.
4 You mustn't smoke.
5 You can/may pass either side.
6 You must/have to be careful (danger!)
7 You can/may camp here.
8 You must / have to switch off mobile phones.
9 You mustn't drink this.
10 You mustn't drive faster than 20 kph.
11 You can/may park here.
12 You can/may smoke here.
13 You can/may cross the road here.
14 You must / have to turn left here.
15 You must / have to put out campfires.
16 You must / have to drive slowly.
17 You can/may cross the road now.
18 You mustn't take photographs here.
19 You can/may wait here for the bus.
20 You mustn't run here.

Original meanings (Box 9.7)

1 Press; interview room	11 Protection and safety equipment
2 Keep frozen	12 Agitate
3 Open door or lid	13 Rendezvous point
4 Dry; heat	14 Tourist activities
5 Blood donors	15 Paediatric clinic
6 Internet and email facilities	16 Water sports area
7 Registration	17 Slow
8 Lock (on river or canal)	18 Amphitheatre
9 Lost child	19 Spin drying
10 Turning basin	20 Nature trail

9.8 Dilemmas

Focus	All kinds of modals to express possibilities, obligation or necessity
Age	Teenager–Adult
Level	Intermediate–Advanced
Time	20–30 minutes
Preparation	A brief description of a dilemma shown on the board or copied for students (see *Box 9.8* for some examples)

Procedure

1 Present the situation, and make sure it is clear to all students.

2 Ask students to brainstorm comments, suggestions or questions in order to suggest possible, advisable or necessary courses of action.

3 Note briefly on the board all the suggestions.

4 Discuss the ideas with the class, and erase the less practical/useful ones. Perhaps try to decide together which is the best.

Note

The verbs to be used may be dictated in advance: *must* or *have to*, *should* or *ought to*, *may*, *might* or *could*. Or the formulation of ideas may be left open to the students: the task will tend to generate modals anyway.

Variation

Ask the students to role play the situation in small groups: one of them is the person with the problem, the other members of the group are friends offering advice, support and suggestions. Later, the groups describe the conclusions they reached, orally or in writing.

Box 9.8: Dilemmas

- You have noticed your best friend cheating in an end-of-term exam. You and your friend have always been against cheating, up to now.
- You think your parents prefer your younger brother to you: they buy him more new things and generally discriminate in his favour. If you protest, they get angry.
- A classmate at school has bad breath, and nobody wants to sit near him. You don't like to tell him to his face that he has this problem, but you feel really sorry for him.
- Your boyfriend/girlfriend said he or she could not come out with you this evening because of work; but you've just seen him or her coming out of a cinema hand in hand with another girl/boy.
- You and your friends are mountain-climbing; you have been caught in a sudden thick fog and are lost.
- Your car has a puncture, and you have just discovered that the spare tyre is flat. You are alone on a lonely road; night is falling.
- Your mother has had a stroke and is semi-paralysed. She hates the idea of going into an institution but needs constant care. You cannot afford a nurse and do not want to give up your job.
- You have been offered a well-paid job by a rich employer and badly need the money; but people have told you that his business is dishonest.
- Your neighbour's young son has just got his driver's licence. You saw him driving recently: he was driving much too fast and narrowly avoided an accident, which would have been his fault. You spoke about it to his mother, but she refused to believe you.
- You felt really ill last night and rang your boss. He was very nice and told you to take the day off. Today, you got up late and now – at 10 am – feel fine.
- You have put on a lot of weight, none of your clothes fit, and your doctor says you must diet. But you feel OK and enjoy your food – also, you have to eat out a lot in your job.

9.9 Being polite

Focus	Modals in polite requests and offers (*Would you (mind) ...?*, *Could you ...?*, *Shall I ...?*, etc.)
Age	Any
Level	Intermediate–Advanced
Time	20–30 minutes

Procedure

1 Discuss briefly the importance of the forms of courtesy in interaction (see *Note*).

2 Present a brief transaction in abrupt, direct commands/questions/comments. For example:

A: Hey, you! Open this door!
B: It's locked. Want me to get the key?
A: Yeah. Get it. Fast.

and discuss how it could be made more polite. For example:

A: Excuse me, could you open this door?
B: I'm afraid it's locked. Shall I get the key?
A: Please, if you wouldn't mind, as quickly as you can.

3 Divide students into groups of four or five, and give each a situation involving getting someone to do something (see *Box 9.9* for some examples).

4 Ask them to compose two similar alternative dialogues. They then perform the dialogues to the rest of the class, with appropriate acting. The dialogues may, of course, be slightly tongue-in-cheek: the abrupt one obviously aggressive, the polite one exaggeratedly ingratiating.

Language tip

It is worth drawing your learners' attention to the fact that these polite expressions using modals are really important in order to make a request really polite: just adding 'please' is not enough. 'Please open the door', for example, sounds more like an order coming from a police officer than a polite request!

Note

In a monolingual class, you might like to take time to compare courtesy forms in the students' L1 with those used in the target language. Note that there might be some forms that don't even exist in one or the other language. (English doesn't have a word for 'bon appetit', for example.)

Variation
To make it easier, you may prefer to compose the original (abrupt) dialogues yourself in advance, and give them to the groups directly – but this makes the exercise rather more mechanical and less creative.

Box 9.9: Being polite

Getting someone to lend you some money
Selling flags or flowers for charity
Getting something to eat in a restaurant
Taking/giving in an assignment
Asking someone to give back something they've borrowed
Asking someone to go out with you
Getting help with lifting something heavy
Getting a noisy neighbour to be quiet
Helping a blind person to cross the road
Asking for directions
Hitching a lift
Booking a room in a hotel

9.10 Deductions

Focus	Modals to express logical necessity or possibilities (e.g. what *must/can't/could/might* be true)
Age	Teenager–Adult
Level	Intermediate–Advanced
Time	30–40 minutes
Preparation	Ask as many students as possible to bring to class photographs of people in their family. These should show the subject in the process of doing something – not static portraits. Bring a similar photograph of someone in your own family.

Procedure

1 Show your photograph, and ask the class to try to deduce whatever they can about its subject. For example:

She must be your mother or sister – she looks like you!
He could be playing football.

2 When students have exhausted their ideas, tell them the true background to the picture.

3 Post their photographs round the class, with a sheet of paper under each one, and invite them to go round writing up their deductions or conjectures, using the same structures they have just used orally. Help individuals where necessary – and contribute your own ideas as well.
4 Read out the suggestions under each photograph, and ask its owner to give the true interpretation.

9.11 Evidence

Focus	Modals to express logical necessity, in both present and past (e.g. what *must/can't* be true; what *must have / can't* have happened)
Age	Teenager–Adult
Level	Intermediate–Advanced
Time	20–30 minutes
Preparation	A set of sentences, cut up, for each pair (see *Box 9.11*)

Procedure

1 Write up a sample sentence on the board. For example:

There must have been a storm last night.

2 Ask students to suggest the evidence that led you to that conclusion. They might say:

The ground is very wet this morning.
There are trees lying on the ground.

3 Note that the hints have to be in the form of concrete evidence, things you can imagine actually seeing or hearing or feeling in the present. So a paraphrase or hint such as 'It was raining last night' is not permitted: you'd have to say how you know **now** (see *Note*, p. 142).
4 Now put the students in pairs. Each pair gets a set of the slips of paper with similar sentences on them. The first student picks up a slip and by providing evidence tries to elicit from his/her partner the sentence on the slip (it doesn't have to be the exact words, as long as they have guessed the situation). Then it is the turn of the second student.
5 If a partner cannot guess, the slip is revealed and discarded. Slips that are successfully guessed are piled up at the side.
6 Stop the process after 15–20 minutes: how many did each pair of students manage to guess between them?

Box 9.11: Evidence

That girl must be ill.	That man must be from the U.S.A.
He must have hurt his foot.	She can't possibly be a dancer.
He must have missed the bus.	It must be time to finish the lesson.
You must have a cold.	That dog must be very old.
The air conditioner can't be working.	That boy can't have washed for some time.
The house must have been burgled in the night.	Someone must have been baking bread here.
The grapes can't be ripe yet.	This room can't have been cleaned for a long time.
She must have run all the way home.	There must be a party at their house.
That child must be lost.	She must have lost her house key.
That woman must be very rich.	That car must have been in an accident.
It must be very cold outside.	Nobody can have lived in that house for a long time.
That boy must be in love.	That television programme must be very funny.
They must have gone to bed very late last night.	Something terrible must have happened.
The lesson must be boring.	I must have offended her somehow.
There must be mice in the house.	You must be very happy!

Note

I have found that some students find it quite difficult to grasp the idea that only *concrete present evidence* will do: they sometimes try to give any kind of hint. It can help to add an interim stage, where you write another sample situation up on the board, with one student who stands with his/her back to it. Then the class suggests all sorts of bits of evidence for the situation. This way you can check that they understand the basic idea before you divide them into pairs.

9.12 Then and now

Focus	*Used to* to refer to past habits or facts that are no longer true (Variation: contrasting past and present modals)
Age	Teenager–Adult
Level	Intermediate–Advanced
Time	30–40 minutes

Procedure

1 Discuss with students how they remember their childhood (in the case of adults, this might include their teenage years).

2 Then ask them to write down as many things as they can think of that they used to do, or that used to be true then, but no longer. For example:

I used to have a dog, Billie.
I used to speak Hungarian with my grandmother.

3 After 10 or 15 minutes of writing (you may need to help with some new vocabulary), ask them to read out some of the things they have written; or they may share their ideas in groups before reporting to the full class.

4 Particularly with a multilingual and multicultural class, students' contributions may develop into interesting full-class discussion and comparison.

Variation

Ask students to list things they could or could not do in the past, but can now; or things they had to do in the past, and don't have to any more.

10 Negatives

10.1 Erasing picture dictations

Focus	Simple negative sentences in the present
Age	Young
Level	Beginner–Elementary
Time	20–25 minutes

Procedure

1 Students dictate to you a simple picture – a scene, a person, a still life – which you draw on the blackboard, adding new features as they suggest them (as in *8.2 Picture dictation*).

2 Then ask them to take the things you have drawn, in any order, and convey to you that they are not there, using simple negative sentences. Whatever they negate in this way, you have to erase. For example, they may have told you originally:

Alice has a hat.
Alice has a feather on her hat.

but now someone may say:

Alice doesn't have a hat.

Whereupon you erase the hat (but may leave the feather hanging in the air!). This goes on until the board is empty.

Note

The negative sentences here will mostly use *have* and *there is / there are* in the negative.

10.2 What's the difference?

Focus	Simple negative sentences in the present
Age	Young–Teenager
Level	Elementary
Time	20–25 minutes
Preparation	Paired pages containing sets of numbered pictures with slight differences (see *Box 10.2a Sets a* and *b* or *Box 10.2b Sets c* and *d*).

Procedure

1 Students work in twos, each having one of a pair of pages. They are not allowed to show each other their pages.

2 The two students tell each other about their pictures and try to work out what the difference is between the pairs. For example:

A: Number one is a girl.
B: Yes, it's a girl.
A: She has a black top.
B: No, she doesn't have a black top, she has a white top.

3 When they have decided what the difference is, they write down the difference as a **negative** sentence. For example:

1B: The girl doesn't have a black top.

4 When the first pair finishes, stop everyone, and elicit answers.

Note

You could make your own sets of pictures, but make sure that the differences are such that they can be easily defined in simple language. Download simple line drawings from the Internet, and – if you don't have the appropriate technology to do it on the computer – print out two copies, and make alterations to one of them with a black pen and/or white-out fluid.

Box 10.2a: What's the difference?

Set a

Set b

Box 10.2b: What's the difference?

Set c

Set d

10.3 Picture differences

Focus	Simple negative sentences in the present
Age	Any
Level	Elementary–Intermediate
Time	30–35 minutes
Preparation	Pairs of pictures with ten differences between them (see *Boxes 10.3a, 10.3b* and *10.3c*). The first pair to be displayed on the board; others copied so that students can work in pairs.

Procedure

1 Display the first pair of pictures, and ask students to find and define differences between them, using **negative** sentences; that is, they must define what is **not** so in one picture (contrasted with what **is** so in another). For example:

> In my picture the man doesn't have a suitcase (but in your picture he has).

2 Distribute one of the other pairs of pictures to pairs of students, so that each member of a pair has a different picture (A or B). Tell them **not** to look at each other's pictures.

3 Tell them that there are exactly ten differences between the pictures; they should try to find as many as they can in ten minutes.

4 Check and tell them any differences they did not find.

Variations

1 An easier variation is to allow each pair of students to look at their pictures openly, without hiding them from each other. But they are not allowed to point to or touch either picture. They then define and write down all the differences they can find, using negative sentences to do so.

2 Instead of specially drawn pictures with a set number of differences, use glossy magazine cut-outs or pictures from the Internet with roughly similar subjects: two advertisements for cars, for example, or two pictures of football players in action. Put each such pair into an envelope, with 'Find five differences' (or whatever number you feel appropriate) written on it. Make up a number of such envelopes, each containing a different pair of pictures. Each pair of students gets a different envelope; when they finish, they get a new one or exchange with another pair.

Box 10.3a: Picture differences

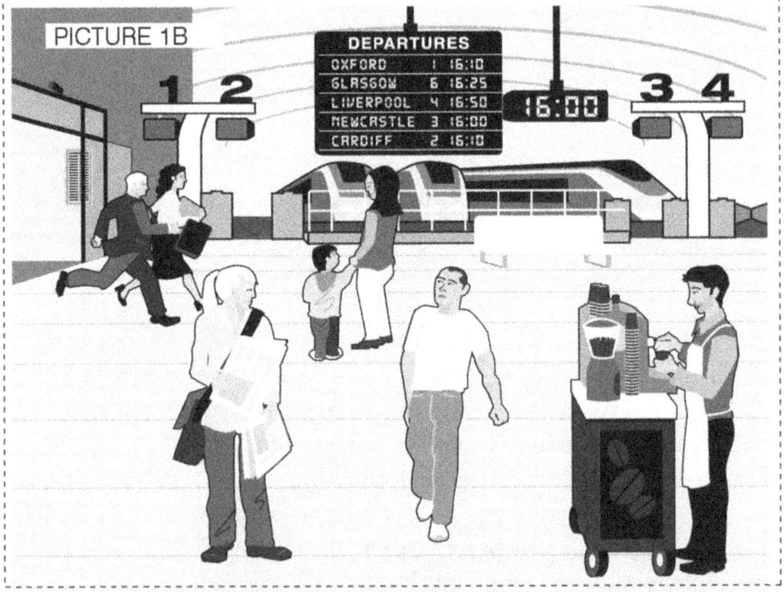

Box 10.3b: Picture differences

Box 10.3c: Picture differences

Answers (Box 10.3a)

1 In picture A the time is not 1600 but 1500.
2 In picture A the screen doesn't say 'Departures', it says 'Information'.
3 In picture B the man in the foreground doesn't have a suitcase.
4 In picture B the man selling coffee doesn't have a cap.
5 In picture A the two people on the left aren't running, they are walking.
6 In picture A the doors on the left aren't open, they're shut.
7 In picture B the man in the foreground doesn't have a dog.
8 In picture B there is nobody sitting on the bench under the clock.
9 In picture B the person selling newspapers isn't wearing a cap OR In picture A the person selling newspapers doesn't have long hair.
10 In picture B the little boy isn't (pointing and) looking at the screen, he's looking to the right.

Answers (Box 10.3b)

1 In picture A there isn't a Parking sign.
2 In picture A the man standing by the road doesn't have fair hair; he has black hair.
3 In picture A the dog isn't sitting, it's standing.
4 In picture A the man crossing the road isn't running, he's walking.
5 In picture A the hand of the man telephoning isn't in his pocket.
6 In picture A there isn't a woman sitting in the car.
7 In picture B the man standing by the road doesn't have a tie.
8 In picture A the car isn't a taxi.
9 In picture B there is no word 'Telephone' on the phone box.
10 In picture B there is no postbox by the phone box.

Answers (Box 10.3c)

1 In picture A there aren't any birds in the sky.
2 In picture B there aren't any numbers on the number plate.
3 In picture B the woman going into the shop doesn't have a bag.
4 In picture A the petrol pumps don't have numbers.
5 In picture B the name of the filling station isn't 'Drake', it's 'Brook'.
6 In picture A the man walking away from the shop doesn't have glasses.
7 In picture B there isn't a man looking under the lorry.
8 In picture B the man filling the car isn't wearing a suit; he is wearing jeans.
9 In picture B the big sign doesn't say 'Turn off engine', only 'No smoking'.
10 In picture B there aren't two children in the car, there's only one.

> **Teaching tip**
>
> In group or pair work in a monolingual class where the students are not under the teacher's direct supervision, they may often wish to use their own language. Some L1 use is of course inevitable and often useful. But if your students are starting to use it too much and unnecessarily, it can help to add an observer to each group who does not participate but simply notes down every time a student uses the L1 – the report being handed to you at the end of the session. The mere awareness that someone is noticing and recording such lapses works as a very effective deterrent!

10.4 Questionnaires with negative answers

Focus	Negative responses to set questions, contrasted with affirmative
Age	Any
Level	Elementary–Intermediate
Time	25–30 minutes
Preparation	Copies of one of the questionnaires based on 'yes/no' questions (see *Boxes 10.4a*, *10.4b* and *10.4c*, or *Boxes 7.1.3a* and *7.1.3b* for other examples)

Procedure

1 Students administer the questionnaires to each other; positive answers may be given as 'yes', but negatives must be given in full sentences.

2 If possible, each student should talk to several other students, and note answers on their questionnaires, using a ✓ to denote a 'yes' and a × to denote a 'no'.

3 Then ask for reports, in the third person, of negative replies that were given, perhaps adding further details if relevant. For example:

Jan doesn't have a healthy diet: he doesn't eat enough fresh fruit and vegetables.

4 Optionally, try to make some generalizations. For example:

Most people in this class don't exercise regularly.
No one has missed work because of illness in the last month.

Box 10.4a: Questionnaires with negative answers

Health By each question fill in a ✓ for 'yes' and a ✗ for 'no'	Name:	Name:	Name:	Name:
1 Have you been to the doctor's in the last six months?				
2 Do you have a healthy diet?				
3 Did you sleep at least eight hours last night?				
4 Do you exercise for at least one hour every day?				
5 Do you spend a lot of time sitting down every day?				
6 Do you laugh a lot?				
7 Have you missed any work/studies because of illness in the last month?				
8. Have you spent more than two weeks in hospital in the last year?				

Box 10.4b: Questionnaires with negative answers

Clothes By each question fill in a ✓ for 'yes' and a ✗ for 'no'	Name:	Name:	Name:	Name:
1 Do you enjoy buying clothes?				
2 Are you wearing something new at the moment?				
3 Do you buy new clothes at least once a month?				
4 Do you think it is more important to be fashionable than comfortable?				
5 Do you enjoy buying clothes for other people (children, a close friend or partner)?				
6 Do you read fashion magazines?				
7 Is it important to you to wear fashionable clothes?				
8 Have you ever bought something and then never worn it?				

Box 10.4c: Questionnaires with negative answers

Children By each question fill in a ✓ for 'yes' and a ✗ for 'no'	Name:	Name:	Name:	Name:
1 Do you enjoy being with children?				
2 Are you an only child?				
3 Are you close to your parents?				
4 Were your parents strict?				
5 Are children today better-behaved than they were ten years ago?				
6 Do you think children should decide whether to go to school or not?				
7 If they go to school, should they choose which lessons they want to go to?				

10.5 Don't say no

Focus Negative answers to questions
Age Any
Level Elementary–Intermediate
Time 10–20 minutes

Procedure

1 One volunteer comes to the front of the class, and the others ask him/her questions, trying to elicit the answer 'no'. The answerer must give true answers but can't say 'no': he/she must find alternative ways of giving negative answers, in full sentences! So answers like 'not really' or 'never' are unacceptable. For example:

A: Does the President of the United States live in Canada?
B: The President of the United States does not live in Canada.
C: Would you like to fail tomorrow's test?
A: I would prefer not to fail tomorrow's test.

'Yes', however, is allowed; so students might slip in some 'yes' questions occasionally in order to lull the answerer's suspicions.

2 When the answerer lets slip a 'no', or has managed to field questions successfully for three minutes without doing so, he/she stands down, and someone else takes his/her place.

10.6 Negative hints

Focus	Negative sentences as definitions
Age	Young–Teenager
Level	Elementary–Intermediate
Time	15–20 minutes

Procedure

1 One student goes out of the classroom; the rest choose an item to be guessed.

2 The student comes back and is given only a very broad hint as to what the item is: 'It's a thing' or 'It's small', for example.

3 The students who know the answer provide the student who doesn't with all sorts of more detailed hints as to what the answer is – but they can only use negative sentences! So the challenge is how to find negative hints that do in fact help the guesser to discover the item. The class might say about a diamond necklace, for example:

It isn't cheap.
It isn't made of glass.
Men don't usually wear it.
You wouldn't wear it to work!

4 If the student is having a really hard time guessing, allow one positive hint. (And then, if necessary, more!)

10.7 Discrepancies

Focus	Negative sentences in the past (Variation: negative sentences in the present)
Age	Young–Teenager
Level	Elementary–Intermediate
Time	10–20 minutes
Preparation	A story that students are familiar with

Procedure

1 Improvise or read out a story to the students which you are sure they all know. This could be a traditional folk tale or a story which you have recently read in class.

2 Introduce obvious mistakes as you go. Every time the students hear a mistake, they raise their hands and offer corrections. For example:

Once upon a time there was a little boy called Goldilocks, who had long green hair ...
It wasn't a boy, it was a girl, and she didn't have green hair ...

Variation

You can base your spoken text on an inaccurate description of a picture that everyone can see or an inaccurate description of things everyone can see in the classroom.

Follow-up

Similar texts may be given in writing for homework; ask students to cross out or underline the erroneous bits and write their corrections below: these should include what was wrong (usually a negative sentence) and what it should be (usually affirmative). Students welcome the opportunity to do some text correction themselves!

11 Nouns, articles and determiners

11.1 NOUNS WITH *A / AN / THE* / ZERO ARTICLE

11.1.1 What's that? Where is it?

Focus	*A/an* and *the* before nouns
Age	Young
Level	Beginner
Time	10–15 minutes
Preparation	A set of toys representing different animals or objects which the students know the words for in the target language; alternatively, pictures of them

Procedure

1 Using a toy frog (or whatever), teach the exchange:

What's that?
It's a frog.

2 Practise until the students know it by heart, and then let them perform it in pairs, using the different items.

3 Take each item in turn and place it in a different place in the classroom saying: 'The ... is here' (and describing the location if you wish: for example 'on the table').

4 Invite one student to the front of the class. Tell him/her to close his/her eyes and then ask 'Where's the ...?' Challenge him/her to point to the location, saying 'It's here' or 'It's there' (or 'It's on the table').

5 Do this again, several times, getting one of the students to ask 'Where's the ...?'

Note

Draw students' attention to the fact that when they were being introduced to the new object, they said 'a' frog; but when they knew which frog was being referred to, they used 'the'. It might be useful to draw students' attention to the difference between *here* and *there*, which is also practised in this activity. This difference corresponds to the distinction between *this* and *that*, which is not found in some other languages.

Variation

Close your eyes yourself, and invite the students to ask you 'Where's the... ?'; see if you can remember!

11.1.2 Expanding headlines

Focus	Insertion of *a/an/the* or nothing before nouns
Age	Teenager–Adult
Level	Intermediate–Advanced
Time	10–15 minutes
Preparation	Copies of a set of fictional newspaper headlines (see *Box 11.1.2*), possibly cut up into separate slips (see *Teaching tip*, p. 160)

Procedure

1 Write up one of the headlines on the board, and ask the students where they would insert *a/an/the* before a noun or noun phrase, and where they would not, if they were expanding the headline into a sentence.
2 Continue with further headlines, or let students select and work on them individually.
3 Check answers yourself; or ask students to check each other's answers, consulting you in cases of doubt. Where there is more than one possibility, discuss the differences between the different versions.

Variation

Instead of the headlines shown in *Box 11.1.2*, use actual headlines cut from English-language newspapers or downloaded from news websites.

Notes

1 It might be helpful to remind those learners whose languages lack one or more of the articles that known items or information would probably be signalled with *the*; new, sometimes vague, information with *a/an* or no article.
2 You will probably need to help a bit with vocabulary here, particularly if you are using the authentic headlines suggested in *Variation*.

Follow-up

Ask students to insert not only missing articles, but also auxiliary verbs that are often omitted (*is/are*, *do/does/did*), or any other items necessary to form complete sentences.

Box 11.1.2: Expanding headlines

1 **Bus in accident**

2 **Sunny days next week!**

3 **King returns to capital**

4 Worst weather since 1988!

5 *Woman gives evidence*

6 Latest research reveals health problem

7 **Suspicious object found in central bus station**

8 *President has new idea for peace*

9 Doctors may use new drug

10 **Dollar rises**

11 ***Problem with new airport terminal***

12 ***All rivers in area may be polluted***

13 Technology key to progress

14 **Unknown runner wins world championship**

15 **Disaster hits Olympic Games**

16 Anti-pollution law delayed by unexpected problem

17 ***US Ambassador to meet Prime Minister***

18 *New development in Middle East*

19 **Miners trapped after underground explosion**

20 **Woman gives birth in helicopter**

> **Teaching tip**
>
> If you are working on a series of very short texts, as in *11.1.2 Expanding headlines*, then here is an economical way of using them that enables each student to work at his/her own pace: if you have 15 such texts on a single sheet, make two or three copies and cut them up into separate slips, so you have 30–45 slips. Put them in a central place in the classroom, and invite the students to each take one, do the appropriate task, and then exchange for a new one as they are ready. Stop them when the first student finishes all 15.

11.1.3 Occupations

Focus	*A/an* with occupations
Age	Any
Level	Elementary–Intermediate
Time	15–20 minutes
Preparation	Copies of the list of hints for each pair of students (see *Box 11.1.3*)

Procedure

1 Choose an occupation without telling the students what it is. Identify the owner of this occupation by a 'unisex' name ('Jan' for example), and give the class a hint that could be true of two or more occupations: 'Jan wears white clothes' (see *Box 11.1.3* for some examples).

2 Invite students to think of as many occupations as they can that would be compatible with this information. For example:

Jan is a doctor.
Jan is a vet.
Jan is a laboratory technician.
Jan is an astronaut.

3 Give each pair of students the list of hints, and ask them to write for each at least one sentence identifying the possible occupation of each character.

4 Elicit some of their ideas in the full class; perhaps add more of your own.

Variations

1 With less advanced students, brainstorm with the class all the occupations they know, and write them up on the board before starting the activity. This list then functions as a 'pool' from which to select occupations.

2 Make two or three copies of *Box 11.1.3* and cut up into separate slips: then run the activity as suggested in the *Teaching tip* above.

Box 11.1.3: Occupations

1 Alex works outside.

2 Corey can drive.

3 Riley sometimes works at night.

4 Jordan uses a computer all day.

5 Jackie had to study at university.

6 Gerry earns a lot of money.

7 Chris likes talking to people.

8 Terry uses tools.

9 Kelly works alone.

10 Kit's work is sometimes dangerous.

11 Lee works in a team.

12 Sammy uses water in his/her work.

13 Morgan uses special equipment.

14 Tracey wears a uniform.

11.1.4 Proverbs

Focus	The zero article before nouns with a general meaning (for learners whose L1 inserts a definite article in such contexts)
Age	Teenager–Adult
Level	Intermediate–Advanced
Time	15–20 minutes

Procedure

1. Write up on the board, or project, a selection of the proverbs shown in *Box 11.1.4*: probably six or seven are plenty.
2. Ask the students to translate them into their own language: if the class shares a common language, then the translations can be written up on the board. If not, then each student writes his/her own translations.
3. Discuss the omission of the definite article before the nouns expressing a general meaning in English (see *Note*).
4. Delete or hide the original English proverbs.
5. Challenge the students to translate their L1 versions back into English.
6. Check and discuss the results.

Note

Many languages which have article systems differ from English in inserting a definite article in such cases, encouraging learners to make mistakes like *'The life is hard' or *'Protect the nature'.

Follow-up

Perhaps spend some time discussing the meaning of individual proverbs and comparing with parallel, or contrasting, ones in the students' own languages.

> **Teaching tip**
>
> The 'double translation' procedure suggested in *11.1.4 Proverbs* is a useful technique when working on grammatical points where the L1 has a different usage that leads to interference problems. It raises learners' awareness of differences between the two languages and helps them avoid errors. I have also found that the actual challenge of translating something into the L1 is – in small doses! – an interesting and absorbing activity for many students.

Box 11.1.4: Proverbs

- Actions speak louder than words.
- All men can't be masters.
- All roads lead to Rome .
- Appearances are deceptive.
- Appetite comes with eating.
- Bad news travels fast.
- Beauty is only skin-deep.
- Beggars can't be choosers.
- Blood is thicker than water.
- Business before pleasure.
- Experience is the best teacher.
- Fine feathers make fine birds.
- Love is blind.
- Honesty is the best policy.
- It's no use crying over spilt milk.
- Let sleeping dogs lie.
- Make hay while the sun shines.
- Many hands make light work.
- Money makes the world go round.
- No news is good news.
- Nothing succeeds like success.
- Speech is silver but silence is golden.
- Still waters run deep.
- Time and tide wait for no man.
- Time cures all things.
- Time is money.
- Truth is stranger than fiction.
- Walls have ears.
- While there's life there's hope.
- You can't teach old dogs new tricks.

11.2 SINGULAR AND PLURAL, COUNTABLE AND UNCOUNTABLE NOUNS; *A/AN/SOME/ANY*

11.2.1 Remembering pairs

Focus	Singular and plural nouns, with *a/an/some*
Age	Young
Level	Beginner–Elementary
Time	10–15 minutes
Preparation	Copies of two sets of pictures (see *Box 11.2.1*) for each pair/group of students

Procedure

1 Show a few sample pictures, and ask students to say what they see. If the object is in the singular, they should use the indefinite *a/an*; if it is plural, they should use *some*.

2 Give each pair or group of students two sets of the pictures, which they scatter face down on the table before them.

3 One student starts by turning up two cards. He/she identifies the items using the appropriate determiner. If they are identical, he/she takes them; if not, he/she replaces them on the table.

4 The next student does the same. All participants try to remember where the cards are so that they can turn up two identical cards and keep them. The winner is the participant with the most pairs.

Note

If you want to practise the zero article before plurals rather than *some*, tell your students to identify the plurals with no article: *children* rather than *some children*.

Teaching tip

When preparing small pictures or texts on slips of paper, it is a good idea to back these with stiff paper and/or laminate them for filing and later reuse with other groups.

Box 11.2.1: Remembering pairs

> **Language tip**
>
> In general, in English, a single final *s* is more often than not pronounced /z/; it's a good idea to tell your students this. They will find that even if they mean to say /z/, it will come out /s/ (correctly!) after an unvoiced consonant, and very easily /ɪz/ after a sibilant. So it's not really necessary to instruct them in complicated rules about the pronunciation of the final 's' in plurals or in the present simple tense.

11.2.2 Piling up stores

Focus	Insertion of appropriate determiners before singular/plural and countable/uncountable nouns
Age	Young–Teenager
Level	Beginner–Elementary
Time	15–20 minutes

Procedure

1 You start off with a sentence such as:

In my kitchen I have a carrot.

2 A student continues:

In my kitchen I have a carrot and some sugar.

3 A second student continues:

In my kitchen I have a carrot, some sugar and some eggs.

4 And so on, each student adding another item until the sentence becomes impossible to remember, or until you decide the class has had enough.

Variation

I usually use food as the topic, because it provides plenty of varied examples of countable and uncountable nouns. But there is no reason why you should not 'pile up' other kinds of things. Other possible starting sentences might be: 'When I go on holiday I will take … ', 'Things you can see in a shopping centre are … ' and 'When I am really rich, I will have … '.

Follow-up

Immediately you have finished one such 'round', ask students to see if they can recall, in writing, all the items mentioned – and see if you can yourself!

11.2.3 Shopping

Focus	*A/an/some/any* before singular/plural and countable/uncountable nouns
Age	Young
Level	Beginner
Time	20 minutes
Preparation	Make enough copies of lists of five simple items(see *Box 11.2.3a*) so that half the class can have a copy of one of the lists: these are the shopping lists. Also, make two copies of the goods to be bought (see *Boxes 11.2.3b* and *11.2.3c*).

Procedure

1 Half the students divide the pictures randomly between them: they are the sellers. The others, the buyers, are each given one of the shopping lists. They then approach the sellers, who do **not** openly display their wares, and request their items.

Do you have any apples? / Do you have a pencil?

Yes, here you are. / No, I'm sorry, I don't have any apples/pencils.

2 After four or five minutes, see who has managed to buy – or sell – most items. Obviously not everyone will manage to buy all their items. Then the buyers and sellers change over, and pictures and lists are redistributed.

Notes

1 For beginners, it's a good idea to teach in advance the simple dialogue shown in *Procedure* above.

2 There is a lot of material to be prepared for this activity; but it can be reused, and I have found the work put into it a good investment (see *Teaching tip*, p. 164).

Box 11.2.3a: Shopping

pencil carrots potatoes book pen	apple milk reading lamp bananas backpack
cap umbrella sugar table sunglasses	plates bread cake chair matches
jacket shirt coffee flowers laptop	alarm clock television orange juice eggs scarf
rice pair of shoes butter penknife bicycle	paper tea chocolate earphones and MP3 player watch

Box 11.2.3b: Shopping

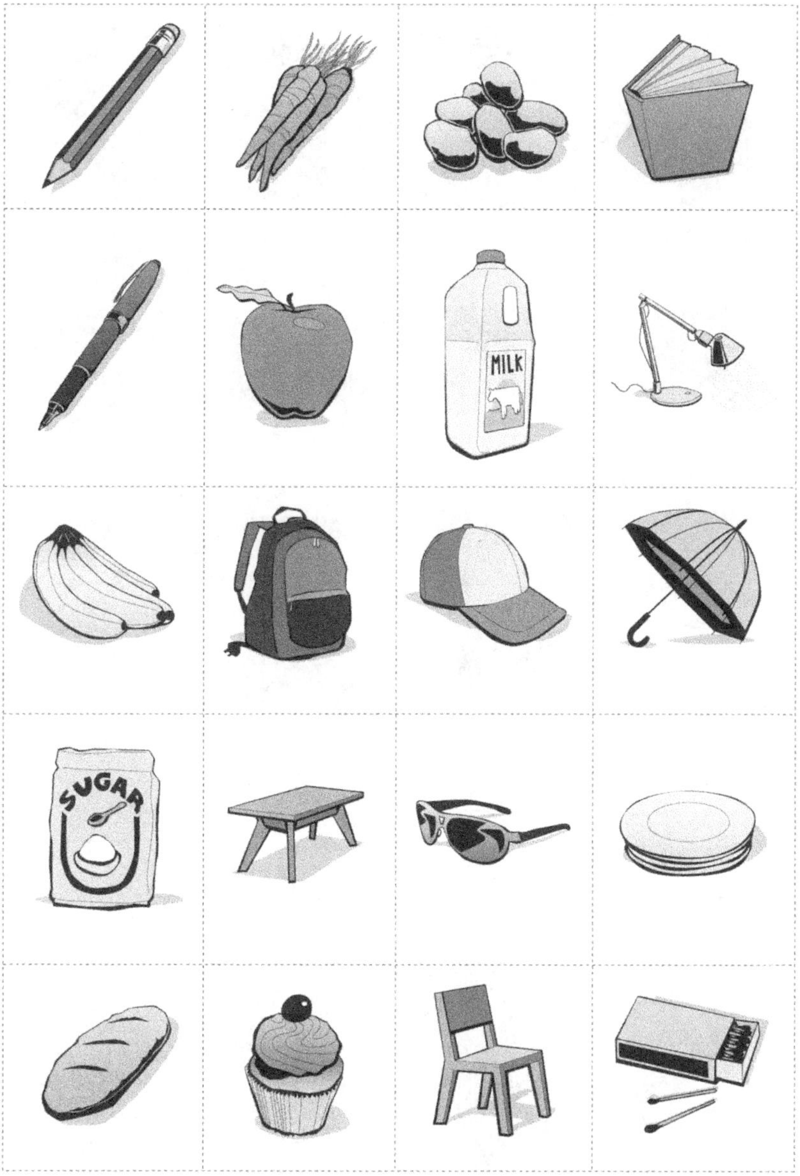

 PHOTOCOPIABLE

Box 11.2.3c: Shopping

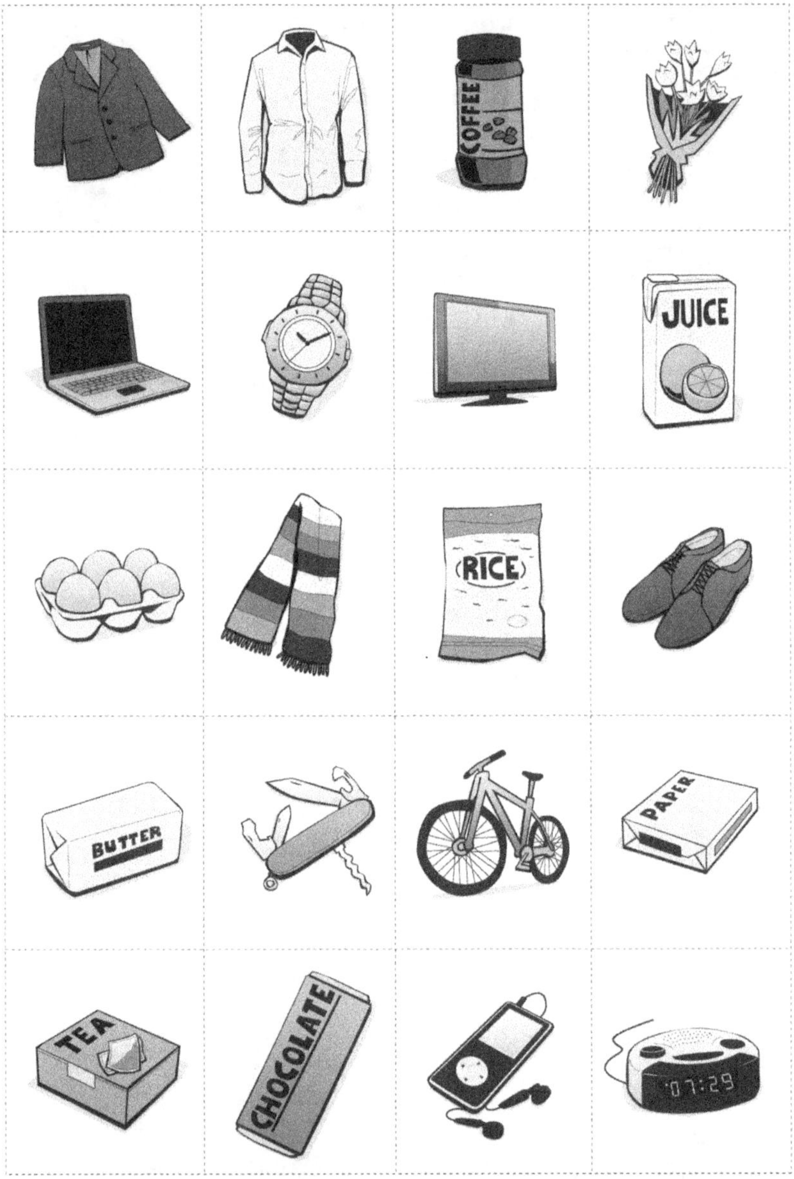

11.2.4 Finding investment partners

Focus	Insertion of appropriate determiners before singular/plural and countable/uncountable nouns
Age	Any
Level	Elementary–Intermediate
Time	15–20 minutes
Preparation	Copies of the table (see *Box 11.2.4a*)

Procedure

1 Show the table, and tell students that each should choose five items only from the list which they would like to buy (invest in).

2 Explain that you are the owner of a shop which can supply these items, but will only do so if there is enough market demand; so in order to make it worthwhile for you to supply an item, each student has to find at least four others who want it as well.

3 Distribute the copies of the tables.

4 Working in 'fluid pairs' (see p. 22), students try to find 'investment partners'.

    I want a/some ... and a/some ..., do you?
    I want a/some ... too, but I don't want a/any ...

5 Students note on their tables who is willing to co-invest with them. A time limit of five or six minutes for this should be plenty.

6 Finally, they report back how many items they can guarantee buying, and that you therefore should supply!

Variation

The things to be bought do not have to be real marketable commodities; students may enjoy doing this activity on the basis of a list of more imaginative 'desirables' – an extra ten years of life, for example, or a perfect figure (see *Box 11.2.4b*).

Note

You may find that you have to make the number of 'co-buyers' larger or smaller, according to the size of your class.

Box 11.2.4a: Finding investment partners

	Partner 1	Partner 2	Partner 3	Partner 4
private cinema				
fast sports cars				
swimming pool				
jet plane				
yacht				
country houses				
penthouse apartment				
diamond jewellery				
tickets for a holiday cruise				
Pacific island				
helicopter				
antique furniture				

Box 11.2.4b: Finding investment partners

	Partner 1	Partner 2	Partner 3	Partner 4
advice on my problems				
more friends				
more time to do things				
more progress in English				
new job				
talent for music or art				
more patience				
peace and quiet				
excitement				
perfect figure				
long life				
happy family				

11.3 *BOTH ... AND ..., NEITHER ... NOR ...*

11.3.1 Association dominoes

Focus	*Both ... and ...*; position of *both* before verb or after *are* (Variation: *so is/does ...*)
Age	Any
Level	Elementary–Intermediate
Time	15–20 minutes
Preparation	A large number of pictures of readily recognizable objects, animals, people: enough for each student to have at least three (see *Boxes 11.3.1a–c*)

Procedure

1. Give each student two or three pictures, and stick another in the centre of the board.
2. The object of the activity is to form an unbroken line of pictures associated with one another from one side of the board to the other.
3. Any student may suggest you take one of his or her pictures for sticking next to a picture already on the board, provided he or she can suggest a convincing point of similarity. For example:

   Both a pencil and a table are made of wood.
   Both a table and a dog have four legs.
4. The rule is that the same kind of similarity may not be used twice; for example, having linked a bag and a car with 'used to carry things', another student may not use the same sentence to link, say, a horse with a car.
5. Students who run out of pictures should be given new ones from a reserve pile.
6. When the line is completed, point to two adjacent pictures and challenge the class to remember the link between them, using 'They both ... ' or 'They are both ... '. And again ...

Note

Some similarities suggested by students may be a bit far-fetched; in cases of uncertainty, you decide whether to accept a particular link or not.

See p. 177 for *Variations*.

Box 11.3.1a: Association dominoes

Box 11.3.1b: Association dominoes

Box 11.3.1c: Association dominoes

Variations

1 Ask the students to formulate their responses as follows:

A pencil is made of wood. So is a table.

A table has four legs. So does a dog.

... in order to cover practice of the *so is/does* ... structure.

2 The same may be done in small groups: if so, then the object is to make a line from one side of a table to the other.

3 An alternative, if the activity is done in small groups, is to play it like a conventional game of dominoes; the object then is to get rid of all your 'dominoes' (pictures), and the participants take turns trying to find a reason to lay down one of their pictures by one already on the table.

11.3.2 Similarities

Focus	*Both ... and ..., neither ... nor ..., both/neither of them* to describe similarities (Variation: *so/neither does/do ...*)
Age	Any
Level	Intermediate
Time	20–25 minutes
Preparation	Copies of the tables (See *Box 11.3.2a*)

Procedure

1 Distribute copies of *Box 11.3.2a*, and ask students to look at the first table ('What they eat or don't eat'). Invite them to suggest similarities between the people using *both ... and* ... or *neither ... nor* ... For example:

Both Jordan and Sindy eat ice cream.

Neither Marta nor Elliot eats fish.

2 Students continue doing the same in pairs or small groups with the second table ('What they can or can't do'). They may be asked to write down their suggestions.

Variations

1 Ask the students to formulate their responses as follows:

Jordan eats ice cream. So does Sindy.

Marta doesn't eat fish. Neither does Elliot.

... in order to cover practice of the *so/neither does/do* ... structure.

2 In pairs, students each get different partially filled tables (see *Boxes 11.3.2b* and *11.3.2c*) and help each other to fill them in by describing who is similar to whom in what respect. They may not show each other their grids and are only allowed to use sentences with *both ... and* ... or *neither ... nor* ...

Follow-up

1 After either the main activity or the variation suggested above, give practice in *both (of them), neither (of them)* by calling out two names from the table and asking the class to identify a point of similarity between them:

Both (of them) eat fish.
Neither (of them) can type fast.

2 Discard the tables completely, and invite students to work in pairs and find as many points as they can that they have in common. They should write these down and later share in the full class, using 'Both of us ... ', 'Neither of us ...'.

Box 11.3.2a: Similarities

1 What they eat (✓) or don't eat (✗)

	meat	ice cream	fish	tropical fruit	salad	pasta
Marta	✓	✗	✗	✓	✓	✗
Jordan	✓	✓	✗	✓	✗	✗
Elliot	✗	✗	✗	✓	✓	✓
Sindy	✗	✓	✓	✗	✗	✓

2 What they can (✓) or can't (✗) do

	drive	speak two languages	type fast	play an instrument	swim
Jade	✗	✓	✓	✓	✗
Don	✓	✓	✗	✗	✓
Sarah	✗	✗	✓	✗	✓
Matt	✓	✓	✗	✓	✗
Katie	✗	✗	✓	✓	✓

Box 11.3.2b: Similarities

Student A					
	drive	speak two languages	type fast	play an instrument	swim
Jade	✗	✓	✓	✓	✗
Don		✓			
Sarah	✗		✓		
Matt				✓	✗
Katie	✗		✓		

Box 11.3.2c: Similarities

Student B					
	drive	speak two languages	type fast	play an instrument	swim
Jade					
Don	✓		✗	✗	✓
Sarah		✗		✗	✓
Matt	✓	✓	✗		
Katie		✗		✓	✓

11.4 *MUCH, MANY, A LITTLE, A FEW, NO*

11.4.1 How much patience?

Focus	*How much / how many*
Age	Any
Level	Elementary
Time	20–25 minutes
Preparation	Eight sheets of paper, each with one of the items from *Box 11.4.1* written or typed in the middle. Make enough copies so that there is one for each pair of students in your class.

Procedure

1 Write up on the board the question and answer:
How much patience do you have? A little!

2 Ask the students what other word they could substitute for 'patience' which would still make sense (and be grammatical!). They can't change the answer. They might, for example, suggest *work* or *confidence* or *money*. But countable nouns like *ideas* would be unacceptable because of the *How much* at the beginning of the question.

3 Write their suggestions above or below the word 'patience' on the board. Elicit about three or four ideas.

4 Put the students into pairs, and give each pair one of the sheets of paper you have prepared.

5 Give each group two minutes to think of at least one alternative to the noun in the sentence and write it under the original. They may add alternative answers as well, to make the whole exchange true of them (or one of them). If they have time to insert two or more alternatives – great!

6 Stop them after two minutes, and tell them to exchange sheets with another pair, and then do the same with the new sheet. Tell each pair to read and correct, if necessary, what the previous pair(s) have already written, before adding their bit.

7 They continue doing the same two or three times more, exchanging with a different pair each time to get sheets they have not yet worked on.

8 Take in the sheets and check.

Follow-up

In the next lesson, read out some of the more interesting contributions. You might also need to discuss any mistakes that were made.

Language tips

1 Note that *much* and *many* are used in negative sentences, but not usually in affirmative ones: You don't normally say 'I have many books / much patience', but substitute other expressions like *plenty of / lots of*. It's probably worth drawing your students' attention to this.
2 The rule about *much/many* is usually defined as relating to uncountable/countable nouns. But a simpler, and equally reliable, rule is that *much* goes with singular and *many* with plural nouns: you don't, in this case, need to talk about 'countableness' at all.

Box 11.4.1: How much patience?

- How much time do you need? Quite a lot!
- How much chocolate do you need to be healthy? Not much!
- How many books do you have? Lots!
- How many students do you know? A few!
- How much sugar is there in your kitchen? A lot!
- How many friends do you want? Just one really good one!
- How many birds can you see in the sky? I can't see any.
- How much paper do we throw out every day? Tons!

11.4.2 Healthy living

Focus	*Plenty, lots of, a lot of, not much, not many, no*
Age	Teenager–Adult
Level	Elementary–Intermediate
Time	15–20 minutes
Preparation	Copies of the list of food (see *Box 11.4.2*)

Procedure

1 Write up four or five of the food items on the board, and invite students to tell you how much of each they would recommend for a healthy, normal diet. They may not use numbers, only expressions like *plenty, lots, a lot of, not much, not many, no*.
2 Divide students into groups, distribute copies of the list, and tell them to decide together how much of each item they would recommend ('not much bread', 'lots of vegetables', etc.). They have to come to a consensus.
3 Share and compare results.

Variation

Ask the groups to decide how their recommendations would change if they were designing a diet for a) someone who wants to lose weight, b) someone who wants to gain weight, or c) a three-year-old child.

Follow-up

Check what the experts recommend here; ask a doctor, nurse or dietician if there is one easily available. Alternatively, tell students to look for an informative website on the subject. Discuss later in class what they have found out.

Box 11.4.2: Healthy living

plenty of, lots of, a lot of, not much, not many, no,

bread	fruit	potatoes	meat	cheese	hamburgers	fish
sugar	eggs	rice	water	steaks	alcohol	fruit juice
milk	coffee	fried food	vegetables	cakes	chips	chocolate

11.5 NOUN MODIFIERS

11.5.1 A business school

Focus	Nouns used as modifiers before other nouns
Age	Any
Level	Intermediate–Advanced
Time	10–15 minutes
Preparation	The list of words (see *Box 11.5.1*) shown on the board or copied for students

Procedure

1 Show the students how one of the items in the list can be combined with another to make a meaningful real-life combination: for example *a business school*, meaning a school that teaches subjects to do with business. Invite them to suggest other combinations and say what they mean.

2 In pairs or small groups, students continue to think up further combinations and write them down. For each, they have to say (but not write) what it means.

3 Elicit some of the resulting ideas.

Note

Remind students that even when the first noun of the combination relates to a lot of things, it is always in the singular: so a shop that sells shoes is a *shoe* (not 'shoes') *shop*. Many other languages use a plural in such combinations, which can lead to mistakes in English.

Variations

1 Challenge them to create further combinations whose meaning is something that doesn't in fact exist or is very unlikely: for example *an apple language* meaning the language spoken by apples, *a book tree*, meaning a tree on which books grow.
2 Add to the list, or substitute, nouns you have recently taught.

Box 11.5.1: A business school

school
shoe
chocolate
book
heart
business
club
language
shop
hotel
tree
room
computer
card
apple
box
luxury
game

12 Numbers

12.1 CARDINAL NUMBERS

12.1.1 Telephone numbers

Focus	Single cardinal numbers
Age	Any
Level	Beginner–Elementary
Time	20–25 minutes
Preparation	Copies of all the names of members of the class, listed vertically

Procedure

1 Each student gets a list and notes down his or her own telephone number by his or her name.

2 One student (or you) begins by announcing his or her own number and asking someone else. And so on. Make sure you speak the numbers slowly, and repeat each number at least twice. For example:

> Hi, this is Penny. My number is 933761. And again: 933761. Jess, what's your number?
>
> Hi, this is Jess. My number is 224365. And again: 224365. Giuseppe, what's your number?

3 Students write the numbers by the appropriate names on their lists.

4 After two or three numbers have been elicited and written down like this, let students walk round the class, asking each other for missing numbers.

5 At the end, check that all the numbers are right.

6 The students now have a list of each others' telephone numbers for future contact!

Notes

1 If students don't want to give their own number, or if you don't think it is appropriate for them to do so, they can make one up.

2 You may need to draw your students' attention to the fact that telephone numbers in English are said one digit at a time: some languages use hundreds and tens in expressing the number.

3 Tell students that they can say 'double two' instead of 'two-two', and so on; but this is optional.

Variation

Instead of lists of names, distribute lists of all the students' telephone numbers (you will need to find these from the school secretary or from the students themselves). There should be no identifying names on the list. Do the same procedure as described above, but students have to identify the numbers and write names by them, instead of the other way round.

Teaching tip

It's good to do some name-learning and getting-to-know you activities in the early stages of a course: this is a very simple example. Other activities that can be used for the same purpose are ones based on personal details, history or tastes such as *7.1.3 Questionnaires*, *7.3.5 Filling in forms*, *1.1.3 The same tastes* and *1.2.5 Preferences*.

Language tip

There are various ways of saying the number '0' in English. In telephone numbers, British English speakers commonly substitute the name of the letter 'O' for this; but perhaps it is best to tell your students to use 'zero' as a universally comprehensible term.

12.1.2 Address book

Focus	Cardinal numbers in addresses
Age	Any
Level	Beginner–Elementary
Time	30–40 minutes
Preparation	In an earlier session, pass round a sheet of paper (or two or three if you have a big class), and ask students to write on it, very clearly, their names, addresses, email addresses and (if you haven't done activity *12.1.1*) phone numbers. Make a copy, on which you blank out all numbers with white-out fluid. Then make copies of this gapped version for students.

Procedure

1 Students fill in the missing numbers in their own addresses, and any others they happen to know.
2 They then go round finding out from each other, and you, all the numbers that they lack.
3 When the first students finish, stop the activity.
4 Read out all the complete addresses yourself, in order to check that everyone has them right, and to give people who didn't finish a chance to fill gaps.
5 At the end, they have an address list for keeping in touch with each other.

Note
Don't do this activity if you feel students would be embarrassed or distressed by having to reveal personal details of this kind.

12.1.3 Number dictation

Focus	Larger cardinal numbers
Age	Any
Level	Beginner
Time	10–15 minutes

Procedure

1 Dictate a series of numbers in the hundreds, in random order, writing them down yourself as you do so.
2 Go on to the next number as soon as the last student has finished writing.

3 Stop after two minutes exactly.
4 Check answers, and then do the same again with another series of numbers; the class tries to break its 'record' for the two minutes.

> **Language tip**
>
> Note that British English speakers add an *and* after the hundreds (*three hundred and fifty*), whereas American English speakers tend not to (*three hundred fifty*). Both are acceptable.

12.1.4 Numbers that are important to me

Focus	Cardinal numbers
Age	Any
Level	Elementary–Intermediate
Time	25–30 minutes

Procedure

1 Check that the students know how to say the years: divided into two numbers (nineteen-sixty); but the first decade of the third millennium one long number (two thousand and one); later back to two numbers (twenty-twelve).
2 Ask the students to write down:
  A year that was important in their lives (e.g. 1998).
  Two other numbers that have personal importance for them.
3 One (volunteer) student reads out his/her numbers; other students ask questions to guess what the significance of the numbers might be.
4 If they haven't guessed, the student reveals the answers.
5 The class divides into groups, and each student displays his/her numbers to the rest. Participants find out about the different numbers and their background stories.

Note

This kind of activity demands a certain intimacy and frankness, and should only be used in a class where the atmosphere is friendly and informal.

12.2 ORDINAL NUMBERS

12.2.1 Significant dates

Focus	Ordinal numbers to express dates
Age	Any
Level	Elementary
Time	15–20 minutes

Procedure

1 Ask students to write down any dates they can remember that have general or national significance: national holidays, major historical events, scheduled occasions this year. They may write them down any way they like: 12 January, January 12 or 12/1.

2 Elicit from students the dates and what they mean: write each up on the board as they are said, with a brief note as to its significance.

3 Draw students' attention to the fact that whereas we normally **write** only '12 January', January 12 or '12/1', we usually **say** 'January the twelfth'or 'the twelth of January'.

4 Now delete the actual dates, leaving only the notes, and challenge students to remember and define the missing dates (the student who suggested the date in question should keep quiet!).

Variation

As with 12.1.4 *Numbers that are important to me*, invite each student to write down a date that has particular significance for him/her (preferably not a birthday, which is too obvious!). Then in groups they try to guess the significance of each other's dates.

Note

It is useful to make a routine of writing up the date on the board every lesson.

Language tip

In the past it was normal to write the date as 'January 12th', with the ordinal number indicated by the 'th': but this is fairly rare these days.

12.2.2 Getting in order

Focus	Ordinal numbers
Age	Any
Level	Elementary
Time	10–20 minutes

Procedure

1 Put students in a line; then ask them to rearrange themselves according to the dates of their birthdays – the one nearest to 1 January at one end, the one nearest to 31 December at the other.

2 Having done that, each one should find out which number he or she is within the class – the third? the tenth? the sixteenth?

3 Then put them into groups of eight to ten students, and ask them to find as many other ways of ranking themselves in order as they can. For example: in length of name or distance we travel each morning to get here.

4 The groups tell each other some of their more original ideas for rankings – and the order they put themselves in.

Language tip

It's worth drawing your students' attention to the fact that ordinal numbers are commonly (though not always) preceded by the definite object: 'the second' rather than 'second'.

Variation

Groups try to find different reasons for ranking that will give each participant at least one opportunity to be in first place.

13 Passives

13.1 Passives on the Internet

Focus	Passive forms of all kinds
Age	Teenager–Adult
Level	Intermediate–Advanced
Time	20–30 minutes
Preparation	You will need computers with an internet connection.

Procedure

1. Brainstorm with the students all sorts of passive phrases, and write them up on the board: 'was taken', for example, or 'are seen'. Try to get up to about 15 or 20 such phrases.
2. Tell them to type these phrases, between double quotation marks, into the 'search' box of Google™, and see what contexts they can find on the Net.
3. They should discard any contexts or sentences they don't understand, and of those that they do understand, they should choose the most interesting one for each phrase and write it down.
4. Share and discuss results: you may find some interesting news items to talk about, or useful collocations and 'chunks' to teach (*taken literally*, for example, or *taken out of context* or *seen as*).

Notes

1. If you wish to focus on practising the irregular passive forms, then limit the initial brainstorm to these forms.
2. Most of the examples the students will have found will be without an agent ('by ...'). Draw their attention to this: the passive in English occurs most frequently without an agent. When there is one, the use of the passive with *by* has the effect of emphasizing the agent.

> **Language and teaching tip**
>
> Many other languages use the passive much less than English does: it is a useful exercise to ask students to translate any passive sentence they are working on into L1, and see if it would more naturally be expressed in their own language by an impersonal active verb form. If so, then they should be aware that when expressing themselves in English, they often need to use a passive where they would use an active in L1.

13.2 What is done – and who by?

Focus	Present passive sentences, with and without the agent
Age	Teenager–Adult
Level	Intermediate–Advanced
Time	15–20 minutes

Procedure

1 Give the students the name of an institution or centre of activity that they know of: for example, the school, a shopping centre, a sports stadium, a street, a hotel, an airport – and ask them to list all the things that *are* normally *done* at this location. Write up their suggestions on the board. In a hotel, for example, they might say:

Credit cards are accepted.
Food is eaten.
Meals are served.
Guests are welcomed.

2 Ask them to identify who these things are done by. Each student writes down the name of an agent suitable to each sentence (you may need to supply some new vocabulary here); then compare and discuss. For example – who are credit cards accepted by? Who is food eaten by?

> **Language tip**
>
> The form *by whom* is used in very formal texts: but *who … by* is more common today in speech and informal writing.

13.3 Describing changes

Focus	Passive sentences in the present perfect (Variation: various other tenses)
Age	Any
Level	Intermediate–Advanced
Time	20–30 minutes
Preparation	Pairs of pictures showing a situation or place before and after a set of changes (see *Boxes 13.3a, 13.3b* and *13.3c* for some examples), shown on the board or copied for students

Procedure

1 Choose one pair of pictures, and display them or distribute copies.

2 Teach or review some of the vocabulary students might need to describe them.

3 Ask the students to imagine that the second picture is the present and to describe, orally or in writing, what *has been done* since the first. For example:

A town has been built.
Water has been brought to the desert.

Variations

1 Tell students they are located in time between the first and second pictures, and need to describe what *is being done* to bring about the changes.

2 Show only the first picture of one of the pairs in *Boxes 13.3a, 13.3b* and *13.3c*, and ask students to predict what changes *will be made* – or, in the case of the untidy room, *should be / need to be made*. Write up all suggestions, then display the second picture: how much did they get right? What did they miss?

3 Discuss the local situation: changes that *have been made* over the last few years, things that *are going to be done* in the future. Ask students to tell you the changes that seem to them to be for the worse, or for the better. Or what they think *needs to be / should be done* – *will* it in fact *be done*?

Box 13.3a: Describing changes

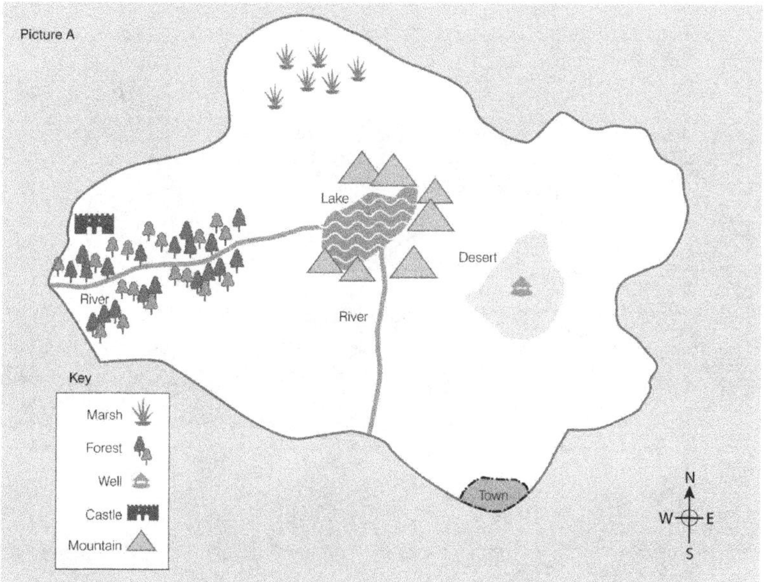

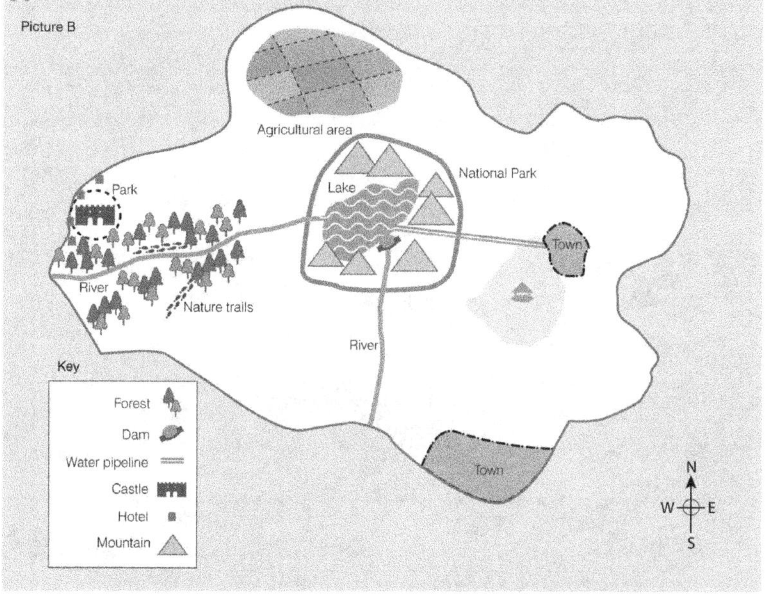

Box 13.3b: Describing changes

Box 13.3c: Describing changes

13.4 Writing it up

Focus	Past simple passive for formal description of a process
Age	Teenager–Adult
Level	Intermediate–Advanced
Time	30–40 minutes

Procedure

1 Discuss with the class how you would describe a process involving a series of operations – such as a science experiment – using the present simple passive, and write up such a description with them. For example:

The equipment was set up ...
A litre of water was heated ...

2 Then ask each student to choose one such experiment or other research procedure he or she is familiar with and describe it similarly, in writing.

3 After writing out their descriptions, students get together in pairs to teach each other about 'their' research and to check the quality of their own reports. Are these clear enough to be followed by a layman?

4 When you have checked their descriptions, the more interesting ones can be read out.

Note

The passive is not appropriate for the description of everyday domestic processes (washing, cooking, etc.), which would most naturally use the active. So this procedure is most suitable for science or academic classes.

13.5 What's being done?

Focus	Present progressive passive to describe a process going on at the time of speaking
Age	Any
Level	Intermediate
Time	15–20 minutes

Procedure

1 Suggest a few things that *are being done* at the present moment within, say, a kilometre radius of the classroom. For example:

The road is being mended.
Cars are being driven.

2 Divide the class into groups, and ask each group to list as many different such activities as they can in five minutes. Which group has the most ideas?

13.6 Election campaign

Focus	Future passive to express promises
Age	Teenager–Adult
Level	Intermediate–Advanced
Time	About 90 minutes

Procedure

1. Tell the students they are preparing part of a candidate's campaign for election to a post in either national or local government. What sort of things should their candidate promise in order to gain votes? For example:

   The main road in this town will be widened.
   A new school will be built.
   More jobs will be provided for young people.
2. Elicit a few such suggestions from the class, and write them on the board. Then divide the class into groups, each of which is supporting a different candidate: they work out a programme of what *will be done* if their candidate is elected and write it out. Supply new vocabulary as asked for, and write it on the board.
3. Then the 'candidates' (role played by one member of each group) present their programmes, supported and prompted if necessary by members of their group.
4. Finally, one of the candidates may be selected by the class in an election (participants are not allowed to vote for 'their' candidates).

13.7 It can be done

Focus	Present passive with modals
Age	Any
Level	Intermediate
Time	20–25 minutes

Procedure

1. Choose a simple inanimate object, and tell all the class except one student what it is.
2. Students describe it by saying what *can be done* with it, until the one who does not know can guess. For example, an egg might be described by sentences like:

   It can be eaten.
   It can easily be broken.

Notes

1 This is a good opportunity to teach and practise the placing of the preposition at the end of a sentence as in 'It can be painted on'.

2 See some guidelines on guessing games in general at *7.1.1. Guessing*.

Variation

You can expand this to use other modals too: for example 'It must be eaten fresh', 'It must be kept in a cool place'.

13.8 By men, by women, or by both

Focus	Present simple passive with agent
Age	Teenager–Adult
Level	Intermediate–Advanced
Time	30–40 minutes

Procedure

1 Ask students to think of five things that are normally, or more usually, done by men, five that are normally done by women and five that are normally done equally by both. Note that they are not required to talk about gender equality, or what would be desirable, at this point, but should simply describe the situation honestly as they see it. For example:

Taxis are usually driven by men.
Houses are usually cleaned by women.

2 In groups, or in full class, share ideas: do they agree with each other?

3 Then discuss in the full class which of the situations they agreed on should be changed so that the activities could be done by both, which should not, and why.

14 Past tenses

14.1 PAST SIMPLE

14.1.1 Recall and share

Focus	Irregular past forms
Age	Any
Level	Elementary
Time	10–15 minutes
Preparation	A set of 10 or 12 irregular past simple forms that you want to practise

Procedure

1. Write up or show the past forms on the board, and tell the students that you are going to erase them and they have to try to remember them all afterwards and write them down.
2. After a minute, erase or hide the items, and challenge students to write down as many as they can remember, each one on their own, without sharing.
3. When they have written as many as they can remember, they share with a neighbour (or two or three neighbours) and try together to recall and write all the items, checking each other's spelling as they go.
4. Finally, write up again, or reveal, the original items. Did they get them all?
5. Check that the meanings of all the items are understood.

Note

This is a neat activity for practising any set of vocabulary items.

Teaching tip

Irregular past forms are theoretically grammar, but for teaching purposes they can be presented and practised as vocabulary. There is no substitute, really, for the old-fashioned method of studying and learning lists of such items as a preparation for any of these activities!

14.1.2 Listening to stories

Focus	Past simple for narrative
Age	Young–Teenager
Level	Elementary
Time	10–20 minutes

Procedure

1 Tell the students a story in the past tense (see *Teaching tip*, p. 70). The story should have plenty of action and be relatively easy for students to understand: possibly a personal anecdote, a traditional folk tale or a story from their textbook.

2 Get students to notice the past forms by asking occasionally for a translation of an irregular form or by stopping and getting them to guess the coming verb – but not so often as to interfere with the pace and momentum of the story.

Follow-up

After you have finished, ask students to recall some of the sentences in the past that were mentioned in the story – using one-word cues to jog their memories.

Note

You don't have to finish a single story in one session; use longer stories or complete books and read them in serial form, a few minutes each lesson.

14.1.3 Piling up events

Focus	Past simple for describing events
Age	Young–Teenager
Level	Elementary–Intermediate
Time	15–20 minutes

Procedure

1 Give each student a verb in the past tense, selecting from ones you have recently taught and wish to practise (for example: *bought*, *sat*, *stood*, *gave*). Then start a simple chain of events with the sentence:

> Yesterday I went to town, and I bought a loaf of bread ...

2 The first student continues, repeating your sentence but adding a further clause including his or her verb:

> Yesterday I went to town, I bought a loaf of bread, and I **sat** on a park bench ...

The second continues likewise:

> Yesterday I went to town, I bought a loaf of bread, I sat on a park bench, and I **stood** at the bus stop ...

3 The process continues until all the students have contributed, or until the chain becomes impossible to remember.

Follow-up

Immediately after finishing the above procedure, ask students to write down as much as they can recall of the final chain – possibly working in pairs or groups to help each other remember.

Variations

1 As each verb is used, write it on the board, so that students can use the list as cues to help them remember the sequence.
2 Instead of providing verbs in the past tense, give them in the 'base' form, so that students have to work out the past form themselves.
3 Instead of providing verbs to begin with, tell students they may choose their own; but they are not allowed to use a verb that has already been used by someone else.

14.1.4 Chain story

Focus	Past simple for narrative
Age	Any
Level	Intermediate–Advanced
Time	20–30 minutes
Preparation	A set of pictures, cut out from magazines or downloaded from the Internet (see *Boxes 11.3.1a*, *11.3.1b* and *11.3.1c* for some examples). There should be enough so that each student can have one.

Procedure

1 Give each student a picture at random. Take one yourself. Begin improvising a story which brings in your picture. For example, if you have a picture of a bird:

> Once upon a time there was a bird which lived in a tree in a wood in Norway. One day the bird heard people walking in the wood ...

2 When you stop, any student may continue if he/she has an idea how to bring in his/her picture. For example, if a student has a picture of oranges, he/she might say:

... The people wanted to have a picnic. They had lots of food with them: sandwiches, apples, oranges ...

3 Another student continues the same way: the goals are for all students to contribute and all items to be included in a (probably somewhat elaborate and unlikely!) story.
4 If one or more students are left with pictures they don't know how to use to continue the story, all the class may help them with ideas.

Follow-up

The original pictures can be gathered in and then used after the end of the activity to stimulate recall of the various sentences:

Who remembers what happened at this picture?

This memory test also provides extra review of the material.

Variations

1 Students may be given verbs instead of pictures. These can be either in the past form or in the base form for students to derive the past form on their own.
2 Students may be given (or choose themselves) other kinds of words, not necessarily past forms – a good way of practising recently learnt vocabulary.
3 The same activity can be done in class in writing. Each student prepares a personal list of about 15 verbs, and keeps it by him or her throughout the activity. On a separate piece of paper each student writes the opening sentence of a story, using the first verb on his or her list, and then passes the paper to a neighbour. On the papers they have just received, students write a continuation of the story (one sentence), using another verb on their list – and so on, until all the verbs are used up. Stories are then read out.

14.1.5 Pictures into story

Focus	Past simple for narrative
Age	Any
Level	Elementary–Intermediate
Time	25–30 minutes
Preparation	Simple picture stories (see *Boxes 14.1.5a*, *14.1.5b* and *14.1.5c* for some examples) shown on the board or copied for students

Procedure

1 Ask students (individually or in pairs) to write down the story represented by the pictures – in the past tense, of course.
2 Three or four volunteers read out their stories.

Teaching tip

When all the students have been asked to do similar tasks, it may sound boring to have them read out their results to each other: but in fact students are often more interested in hearing what their classmates have done with similar tasks than in hearing about different ones that they have not tried themselves.

Variation

Display only the first picture, get the students to start telling the story, and then let them brainstorm ideas as to what happened next. Show them the next picture, let them describe the events it shows (were their guesses right?), and continue similarly with the later pictures.

Box 14.1.5a: Pictures into story

Box 14.1.5b: Pictures into story

Box 14.1.5c: Pictures into story

14.1.6 Putting stories in order

Focus	Past simple for narrative
Age	Any
Level	Elementary–Intermediate
Time	30–40 minutes
Preparation	Sets of pictures copied for students, apparently showing a story – but ambiguous: the pictures could be taken in any order (see *Boxes 14.1.6a*, *14.1.6b* and *14.1.6c*)

Procedure

1 Put students into small groups of three or four, and give each group a set of the pictures cut up.
2 The groups decide in what order they want their pictures to be and write an appropriate story.
3 Each group in turn then reads out a story they have written. As they do so, other groups arrange the pictures in the order they think the story implies. Check they all have the right order before going on to the next story.

Follow-up

Discuss whether there is a 'best' or 'most probable' order of the pictures.

Box 14.1.6a: Putting stories in order

Box 14.1.6b: Putting stories in order

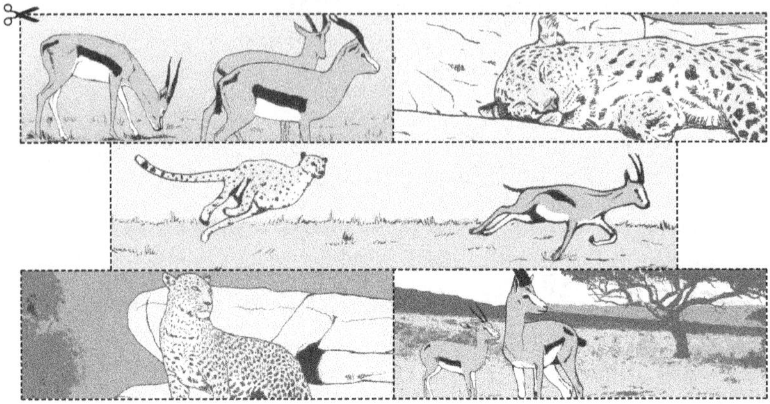

Box 14.1.6c: Putting stories in order

14.1.7 Cooperative story

Focus	Past simple for narrative
Age	Any
Level	Elementary–Intermediate
Time	15–20 minutes
Preparation	Copies of a set of 15–20 words or expressions that you have recently taught in class, or any set of random vocabulary items

Procedure

1. Distribute the list of vocabulary, and explain that the students have to make up stories, in the past tense, that include all the items or as many as they can.
2. Put the students into groups: they start composing their stories orally (they should not attempt to write them down). The stories may be as far-fetched or absurd as they like: the main point is that there should be a clear plot, and that as many as possible of the vocabulary items should be included.

Notes

1. This activity produces a lot of laughter, as the participants make up ridiculous events in order to create contexts for their items. It is, of course, also an excellent activity for vocabulary review.
2. Don't try to have students share results later: they will not be able to remember everything, and the main point is the actual process of telling the stories in the past.

Teaching tip

When students are working in groups, there is always a tendency for one or two to dominate and for others to remain silent. Three tips here: first, keep groups small (not more than four, preferably two or three, students); second, make it part of the instructions that each member of the group has to contribute at least three sentences; third, put active students in a group together with active students, and quieter with quieter.

14.1.8 Changes in your life

Focus	Past simple to describe personal experiences; questions and answers
Age	Teenager–Adult
Level	Intermediate–Advanced
Time	20–30 minutes

Procedure

1 Tell the students about an event in your life that made a big difference to you. For example:

I went to study at a university a long way from home.

2 Encourage them to ask questions, which you answer. For example:

What did you study?
Where was the university?

3 Ask them to think of similar experiences in their own lives and tell the class about them, with follow-up questions and answers.

Variation

The same can be done in small groups. Volunteers can then describe their experiences (or those of other students in the same group) to the full class.

14.1.9 Story behind a photo

Focus	Past simple questions and answers
Age	Any
Level	Intermediate–Advanced
Time	20–30 minutes
Preparation	Ask students in advance to bring to the classroom photos of themselves (preferably not passport or studio portraits) or of a place or people they know. Bring one yourself.

Procedure

1 Show the students your photograph, and tell them something about the circumstances in which it was taken. For example:

I was 16 in this photo; it was my birthday.

2 Students ask questions in order to elicit further detail. For example:

Who took the photo?

3 Invite another student to display his or her photograph and discuss it in the same way.

Note

The photographs do not have to have been taken very long ago! A picture of a student last week at a party, for example, is fine.

Follow-up

Students write brief essays in the past about events or background situations relevant to their photographs.

14.1.10 Alibi

Focus	Past simple questions and answers
Age	Any
Level	Elementary–Intermediate
Time	20–30 minutes

Procedure

1 Select a scene and time for a crime – say, a bank robbery, at a well-known bank in the middle of town, at 11 o'clock yesterday.

2 Two students are the 'suspects' – they are sent outside and instructed to prepare an 'alibi' for one another. This means they have to invent and be prepared to describe a situation during the period of the crime, in which they were in each other's company and can therefore vouch for each other's innocence. For example, they were shopping together, or walking in the country.

3 Meanwhile, the class, who are the 'detectives', prepare a number of questions to ask them.

4 After about five minutes of preparation, the first suspect is called in and asked questions about his or her movements and actions during the crucial time. Then the second. If they do in fact corroborate each other's stories, they are 'innocent'; but if there are inconsistencies and contradictions, they are 'guilty'.

Note

Some of the questions may naturally be in the past progressive.

14.1.11 Interrupt me!

Focus	Past interrogatives
Age	Any
Level	Elementary–Intermediate
Time	10–15 minutes
Preparation	Any story to tell orally: a folk tale, a personal anecdote, a joke

Procedure

1 Tell the students that you are going to tell them a story and they have to try to stop you getting to the end of it by raising their hands and interrupting with questions which you have to answer before going on. The questions must be relevant to the story and must be correctly formed. For example:

One day last week I ... yes, Carlos?
Which day was it?
It was Wednesday. I decided to ... yes, Maria?
What time was it on Wednesday?

2 If the activity is successful you may have to stop them asking, eventually, in order to complete your story!

14.2 PAST PROGRESSIVE

14.2.1 What were you doing?

Focus	Past progressive to describe a past period of activity
Age	Any
Level	Intermediate–Advanced
Time	10–15 minutes
Preparation	A set of pictures of simple objects (see *Boxes 11.2.1a*, *11.2.3a*, *11.2.3b* or *11.2.3c* for some examples)

Procedure

1 Each student gets a picture and decides what he or she was doing (in his or her imagination!) at a given time yesterday evening – say, at eight o'clock: the activity must involve the item depicted.

2 Each student shows his or her picture and says what he or she was doing. A student with a picture of a vase might say:

At eight o'clock yesterday evening I was putting flowers in a vase.

One with a picture of a loaf of bread might say:

At eight o'clock I was making sandwiches.

Follow-up

1 The students then have to find companions. They go round asking:

What were you doing at eight o'clock last night?

If two or more students find that they were doing activities that could 'go together', they join up. For example, someone who was making sandwiches and someone putting flowers in a vase could go together: they might have been preparing for a party.

2 Gather in the pictures and stick them up on the board. Point to each in turn – can the students (not the one whose picture it was!) recall who was doing what with it?

Variation

Instead of using an obvious activity associated with the object, students try to think of an unusual one: for example, a student with a vase might say:

I was drinking coffee out of my vase.
I was selling my vase to a friend for $2,000.

Optionally, you may then ask some of the students then to justify this unusual action, possibly using the past perfect:

I was drinking coffee out of my vase because I'd dropped all my cups.
I was selling my vase for $2,000 because I'd found out it was valuable.

14.2.2 Are you a good witness?

Focus	Past progressive to describe a given past situation
Age	Any
Level	Intermediate–Advanced
Time	20–25 minutes
Preparation	A picture depicting a large number of things going on – a scene in a street, for example, or in a bus station, or in the living-room of a large family (see *Boxes 14.2.2a*, *14.2.2b* and *14.2.2c* for some examples)

Procedure

1 Tell the students you are going to give them a test to see if they are good witnesses or not. They will have to look at a scene and then recall details in response to questions.

2 Show them the picture for two minutes, then hide it.

3 Write up on the board

What can you tell me about ... the baby? ... the man?

and so on, giving five or six of the characters shown in the picture.

4 Students write down their answers. For example:
The baby was playing.
The man was sitting on an armchair.
5 Try answering in writing yourself (without peeping!).
6 Then show the picture again, and let students self-check.
7 What did they (and you!) get wrong or right? Are they/you good witnesses?

Variations

1 In a more demanding version, students are asked to write down everything they can remember that was going on in the scene. Or they can work in groups, pooling their knowledge and composing a written account together.
2 The students themselves may provide the original material for recalling, by setting up a living tableau (arranging themselves in stationary poses, as if they were engaged in different actions or states in a given context). Groups prepare more or less dramatic tableaux, hold them stationary for a minute or two – and then challenge the other students to recall what each member of the group was doing.

Box 14.2.2a: Are you a good witness?

Box 14.2.2b: Are you a good witness?

Box 14.2.2c: Are you a good witness?

14.2.3 When it happened

Focus	Past progressive contrasted with past simple
Age	Adult
Level	Intermediate–Advanced
Time	5–10 minutes

Procedure

1 Recall a dramatic national or international event in the lifetime of the students.

2 Ask each one to say what he or she was doing when it happened or when they heard about it. For example:

When I heard that Princess Diana was dead, I was driving to work.

14.2.4 Begin a story

Focus	Past progressive contrasted with past simple
Age	Any
Level	Intermediate–Advanced
Time	20–30 minutes

Procedure

1 Tell the students they are going to have a competition: who can write the most exciting first paragraph to a story? The condition is that the story has to open with a dramatic event, against the background of some clearly described situation; and the paragraph has to be between 50 and 60 words long.

2 Students work in pairs to devise their story-beginnings: the first few sentences should describe the setting (what *was going on* before the event); the final sentence should say what then *happened*.

3 Students have 15 minutes to do this. Anyone who finishes early may continue the story.

4 The stories are read out. The class decide which was the most exciting opening.

Follow-up

The students continue and finish their stories, to be shared in a later lesson.

14.3 PRESENT PERFECT

14.3.1 Find someone who ...

Focus	Present perfect (questions and statements) with *ever, never*
Age	Any
Level	Intermediate–Advanced
Time	10–15 minutes
Preparation	Copies of a questionnaire (see *Box 14.3.1*)

Procedure

1 Propose a 'Find someone who' task similar to those on the questionnaire. For example:

Find someone who has ridden an elephant.

and ask round the class:

Have you ever ridden an elephant?

until you find someone who has or until it is apparent that nobody has.

2 Write up on the board:

Karen has ridden an elephant.

or:

No one in the class has ever ridden an elephant.

3 Distribute one of the questionnaires, and tell students to try to find at least one person in the class who can say 'Yes, I have ...' for each of the questions and to write down their name.

4 Ask students to tell you at the end what they have found out. For example:

Karen has eaten a frog.
No one has ever slept in a cave.

Follow-up

Invite students to think up similar items of their own. These can be submitted to you and used as the basis for a new questionnaire. Alternatively, invite students to go round asking each other their new questions, and share the results later in informal class discussion.

Variation

Use only the first five or six items of the questionnaire for a shorter and easier activity.

Box 14.3.1: Find someone who ...

1 Find someone who has written a letter to a newspaper.

Name: ________________________

2 Find someone who has read *Harry Potter and the Deathly Hallows*.

Name: ________________________

3 Find someone who has eaten a frog.

Name: ________________________

4 Find someone who has slept in a cave.

Name: ________________________

5 Find someone who has been to Disneyland®.

Name: ________________________

6 Find someone who has spoken to a famous person.

Name: ________________________

7 Find someone who has done all their homework this term.

Name: ________________________

8 Find someone who has broken a bone.

Name: ________________________

9 Find someone who has driven a tractor.

Name: ________________________

Language tip

It is acceptable these days, in informal speech and writing, to use the simple past with adverbs like *ever, never, already, not … yet, just*: 'Did you ever ride an elephant?', 'I just had an amazing experience.' This is standard American usage even in formal language, and is becoming increasingly common worldwide.

14.3.2 What has happened?

Focus	Present perfect to describe events leading to a present situation
Age	Any
Level	Intermediate–Advanced
Time	10–15 minutes
Preparation	Two pictures (see *Boxes 13.3a, 13.3b* and *13.3c* for some examples) showing the same place before and after changes, shown on the board or copied for students

Procedure

1 Choose one of the pairs of pictures, and show them on the board, or distribute copies to students.

2 Tell students that the second picture represents the present situation. Ask them to write down ideas about what *has happened* since the first picture to create these changes. (To provide names: tell them that the owner of the untidy/tidy room is called Kim; the kitchen table is owned by Elly and Jon; the island is being developed by the government, who can be called simply 'They'.) For example:

   Kim has turned off the television.
   They have built a new town.

3 After five minutes' writing, stop the students and elicit ideas.

Variations

1 Tell students that the first picture is the present and the second represents changes that are yet to be made. Ask them to define what *has not yet happened.*

2 If you want to practise the passive of the present perfect, tell them that we don't know who has made these changes; therefore we have to say things like:

   The television has been turned off.
   A new town has been built.

3 Use only one picture, showing a more or less dramatic situation (see *Boxes 4.1.3a–f* for some examples). Students describe what *has happened* to produce the situation depicted. Then ask them to continue with what they think may happen but *has not yet happened*. Again, the same may be done in writing.

14.3.3 Oh!

Focus	Present perfect to describe events leading to a present situation
Age	Any
Level	Intermediate–Advanced
Time	15–20 minutes
Preparation	A set of exclamations (see *Box 14.3.3* for some examples) shown on the board or copied for students

Procedure

1 Show or distribute copies of the series of exclamations, and ask students what they think has just happened to make the speaker say them. For example, 'Oh!' might mean that:

She has had a surprise.

or:

He has just remembered something.

2 Elicit a couple of examples to serve as models, and then tell students to write down what they think has just happened for as many of the exclamations as they can. Give them about ten minutes to do this.

3 Invite a student to read out one of his /her sentences **without** telling the rest of the class what the exclamation was that gave rise to it.

4 The rest of the class (and you!) try to guess which exclamation was intended.

Note

In my experience this activity is likely at some point to produce laughter. If a student has produced the sentence 'I've just got married', for example, based on the exclamation 'Congratulations!', there is usually a humorist in the class who will suggest that the appropriate response is 'What a shame!' or 'Never mind!'.

Variation

To make this activity a little simpler, use only the first 20 exclamations in *Box 14.3.3*.

Language and teaching tip

It is an interesting awareness-raising exercise to look at how other languages express surprise, disappointment, approval and so on. Ask your students what the idiomatic equivalents of some of these exclamations are in their own languages, and compare to English.

Box 14.3.3: Oh!

1	Oh!	**11**	Great!	**21**	(sigh)
2	Wow!	**12**	What a shame!	**22**	No, thank you!
3	Oh good!	**13**	I'm sorry!	**23**	Rubbish!
4	Fantastic!	**14**	Oh no!	**24**	Thank goodness!
5	Congratulations!	**15**	Yes!!!	**25**	Touch wood!
6	Cool!	**16**	Yes?	**26**	Well?
7	Yes, please!	**17**	Hallo!	**27**	Unbelievable!
8	What?	**18**	Never mind!	**28**	Bad luck!
9	Stop it!	**19**	Thank you!	**29**	Cheers!
10	Ouch!	**20**	Welcome!	**30**	Goodbye!

14.3.4 Accounting for moods

Focus	Present perfect to describe events leading to a present situation
Age	Teenager–Adult
Level	Intermediate–Advanced
Time	20–25 minutes
Preparation	A set of pictures showing people in different moods (see *Boxes 14.3.4a* and *14.3.4b*) shown on the board or copied for students

Procedure

1 Go through the pictures with the students, defining with them the apparent feelings of the person depicted ('happy ... sad ... worried') – you may have several possibilities for each picture.

2 Take one picture, and ask students what they think *has happened* to make the person feel this way. For example:

> She is worried because her young son has not come home yet, and it's very late.

3 Write up a few suggestions on the board.

4 Let students do the same in writing for other pictures, working individually or in pairs. They do not need to take the pictures in any rigid order: let them choose whichever ones they want and do as many as they can in the time you allow them.

5 Elicit students' ideas.

Note

This activity may elicit some present perfect passives in the responses: 'She is shocked because (she has discovered that) her bag has been stolen'.

Box 14.3.4a: Accounting for moods

1

2

3

4

Box 14.3.4b: Accounting for moods

5

6

7

8

14.3.5 Things have changed since then

Focus	Present perfect to define happenings or processes during a period up to the present
Age	Teenager–Adult
Level	Intermediate–Advanced
Time	10–15 minutes

Procedure

1 Describe to the students some of the things that have happened in the world in your lifetime. For example:

> The third millennium has begun.
> The planet has got warmer.
> Many more people have learnt English.

2 Ask the students if they can think of things that have happened or changed in the world within their own lifetimes. Help them by suggesting fields of activity: what has changed in ... fashion? transport? communications? eating habits? entertainment? the political scene? sport? science and technology?

Follow-up

Invite students to make posters using sentences such as 'The world has got warmer' as a basis, with illustrations.

Variation

Suggest that students talk in the same way about changes that have taken place in their own lives, say in the last ten years:

> I have been to China.
> I have learnt how to swim.

14.3.6 The right experience for the job

Focus	Present perfect to express past events with relevance for the present situation
Age	Teenager–Adult
Level	Intermediate–Advanced
Time	30–45 minutes
Preparation	Slips of paper with the names of specific jobs (see *Box 14.3.6*)

Procedure

1 Put the students into groups and tell them that each group is a team who has to interview candidates for a specific job (or for a course leading to such a job) (see *Box 14.3.6*).

2 Tell the teams that they have to plan questions to ask the candidates, eliciting whether they have appropriate life experience and other qualities. At least five of the questions have to be in the present perfect. For example:

   Have you worked ...?
   What have you been doing since you left school?
   Have you ever experienced ...?

   But other questions may be in any other tense/aspect form. For example:

   Can you drive?
   What do you do in your spare time?

3 When all the groups have at least ten questions each, one volunteer student from each group goes to another group to be interviewed.

4 When the interviews are conducted, the interviewee may answer truthfully as him/herself or role play someone else, as they wish.

5 After the interviews, ask the groups whether they would accept the candidate they interviewed and why!

Variation

In a more elaborate version of this, each group runs their interview several times, and students take turns going to other groups to be interviewed. This goes on until all or most of the students have been interviewed. The groups are told they can only take one candidate: who, of those they interviewed, will they choose?

Box 14.3.6: The right experience for the job

- Marriage counsellor
- Carer in a children's home
- Hotel receptionist
- Tour guide
- Zookeeper
- TV presenter
- Wedding planner

14.3.7 I have lived here for ...

Focus	Present perfect or present perfect progressive to describe a past state or process extending into the present, with *since* or *for*
Age	Teenager–Adult
Level	Intermediate–Advanced
Time	30–35 minutes
Preparation	Blank slips of paper, two or three for each student

Procedure

1 Ask each student to write in their notebook four to six (true) facts about themselves in the present tense. Do the same yourself.

2 Write up your own sentences on the board. For example:

I am married.

I am teaching this English lesson!

3 Add present perfect sentences showing *how long* these facts have been so:

I have been married for ten years.

I have been teaching this lesson since eleven o'clock.

4 Give out slips of paper, and tell students to write on each slip one such present perfect (or present perfect progressive) sentence, based on sentences they wrote previously, using *since* or *for*, or possibly *always*.

I have had a cat for two years.

I have spoken French since my childhood.

Each student should write two, or possibly three, slips.

5 Take in the slips of paper, and put them in a pile on your desk.

6 Tell the students to choose one slip of paper each and guess who wrote it. If they have no idea, they should make a random guess anyway, and write down what they think in their notebooks. For example:

Elke has had a cat for two years.

Jehan has always been blonde.

7 Then they put back the slip they have just read, and take another – until most of them have looked at and guessed the authors of about 10 to 15 slips.
8 Finally, go through the slips and find out who the authors really were!

Note
This is a good getting-to-know-you activity.

> **Language tip**
>
> The most common mistake with this use of the present perfect and present perfect progressive is for students to use one of the present tenses instead (*'I am married for ten years', *'I am waiting here since one o'clock'), simply because many other languages normally use a present tense in this context. Making students aware of the difference can help them get it right in English.

14.3.8 What have they been doing?

Focus	Present perfect progressive to describe a past state or process extending into the present or ending shortly before it
Age	Any
Level	Intermediate–Advanced
Time	15–20 minutes
Preparation	Pictures (see *Boxes 14.3.8a* and *14.3.8b*) shown on the board or copied for students

Procedure
1 Display one of the pictures, and challenge the students to say what the characters *have been doing* – and how they know! For example:

> Bob has been swimming: his hair is wet, and he's drying himself with a towel.
>
> Rob and Tim have been fighting: Rob has been pushed over, and Tim has a black eye.

2 In pairs, students work on the pictures and try to account for the recent activities of each character: what has he/she been doing? Note that not all the answers are obvious: there is room for conjecture or alternative possibilities.

Box 14.3.8a: What have they been doing?

Box 14.3.8b: What have they been doing?

14.4 PAST PERFECT

14.4.1 Past diary

Focus	Past perfect to describe events done (or not done) by a specified time in the past
Age	Teenager–Adult
Level	Intermediate–Advanced
Time	10–15 minutes
Preparation	Mickey's diary (see *Box 4.1.1*) shown on the board or copied for students

Procedure

1 Present the diary as showing the events of last week.
2 Pick one day: ask the class what Mickey *had done* by a specified hour of that day.
3 Then tell students to look carefully at the schedules of two days (say, Tuesday and Wednesday) and try to memorize as much as they can.
4 Students should then try to remember what Mickey *had done* by Tuesday night, and what he/she *had not yet done* (would do on Wednesday).
5 Let students look at the diary again: what had they forgotten?

14.4.2 Changes: before and after

Focus	Past perfect to describe events or states before a specified time in the past
Age	Teenager–Adult
Level	Intermediate–Advanced
Time	20–25 minutes

Procedure

1 Think of some period that made a great impression on you: a course of study, an impressive trip, some kind of edifying (or traumatic!) experience.
2 Briefly describe your experience to the class.
3 Tell the students about the difference it made to you, in a sentence or sentences based on the past perfect and the past:

    I had always thought ... but then I found out ...

4 Then ask students to write down their sentences – as many as possible, to express the widest possible implications of their experiences. Supply vocabulary to individuals as needed.

5 Then ask a volunteer student to describe his or her experience and to explain to the class what differences it made to his or her life – using the written sentences as a basis, but amplifying freely.

Variation

Students may tell their experiences to one another in pairs – and then, perhaps, report back to the class in the third person, each student describing the experiences of his or her partner.

14.4.3 True or false?

Focus	Past perfect within indirect speech
Age	Any
Level	Intermediate–Advanced
Time	10–15 minutes

Procedure

1 Each student writes down two fairly unusual or interesting things that have happened to him/her in the past: one should be true and one false. For example:

> I lived in Paris for two years.
> I once saw a cobra in the wild.

2 They read out their sentences to the class.

3 Other students try to recall what other students said and say if they believe them or not.

> Marco said he had once seen a cobra, but I don't believe him.

4 You won't have time, probably, to go through all the students' sentences in this way: continue for about ten minutes, or until you feel the class has had enough.

5 Students reveal the truth about their statements!

Note

This is, of course, an excellent activity for practising the past simple as well.

15 Possessives

15.1 Statues

Focus Possessive determiners with parts of the body
Age Young–Teenager
Level Beginner–Elementary
Time 15–20 minutes

Procedure

1 Review different parts of the body: easy ones such as *hand, finger, head, foot/feet*, but also more advanced ones such as *waist, knee, chin, elbow*. You may need to write some of these on the board.
2 One student comes to the front of the class, and you give him/her three commands such as:

   Put your hand on your head!
   Put your finger on your nose!
   Put your foot on the chair!

3 Ask the student to hold the position while you ask the class: what did he/she do?
4 They answer 'He put his hand on his head' (or 'She ... '), etc.
5 Put the students into groups and tell them to do the same with one of them acting as the human 'statue'.
6 As they finish, they call you over, and you ask them to tell you what the student did, as in step 4 above.

Note

Some languages use the definite article before the part of body in contexts like this, so make sure that the possessive is in fact used throughout.

15.2 Who is lying?

Focus	Possessive determiners *my, your, his, her* (Variation: possessive pronouns *mine, yours, his, hers*)
Age	Young–Teenager
Level	Beginner–Elementary
Time	15–20 minutes

Procedure

1 Tell students you are going to find out how good they are at lie-detecting!

2 Send two students (the potential 'lie-detectors') outside, and ask another student for a small object that belongs to him/her but is not, obviously, labelled with its owner's name.

3 The lie-detectors come back, are given the object and have to try to find out whose it is. One of them asks one of the students:

Is this your pencil?

The student – whether it is in fact his or hers or not – denies it:

No, it's not **my** pencil, it's **her** pencil. (indicating another student)

4 The other lie-detector then asks the student indicated, and so on, until all the students have had a chance to deny ownership.

5 At the end, the lie-detectors confer and decide who they think is the liar. If right, they are congratulated: they obviously have a talent for detection!

6 Another two students take their place and the process is repeated.

Variations

1 To practise possessive pronouns, use the dialogue:

A: Is this yours?

B: No, it isn't mine. It's his/hers.

2 The same basic procedure can be used to practise all sorts of other things: the present perfect, the past, the present simple: see for example *17.1.1 Detectives*.

15.3 Family tree

Focus	Possessive *'s* to indicate relationships
Age	Young–Teenager
Level	Beginner–Elementary
Time	15–20 minutes
Preparation	A diagram of a family tree shown on the board or copied for students. The family tree may be an invented one (see *Boxes 15.3a* and *15.3b* for examples); or use a representation of a family the class know of and can relate to: your own, one of theirs, one from a familiar television series.

Procedure

1 Ask students to define the relationship between any two of the names, using the possessive *'s*. For example:

    John is Fay's husband.
    Matt is Nathan's uncle.

2 As they do so, draw in a coloured arrow connecting the two names mentioned: so from the above suggestions there would be an arrow from John to Fay and from Matt to Nathan. There will sometimes be parallel arrows; for example, a parallel arrow going the other way will be produced by the sentence 'Fay is John's wife'.

3 By the end, every name should be linked to at least two others.

4 Point to any of the arrows, and elicit, orally or in writing, the sentence that it represents.

Variations

1 Put the students into pairs, and give one of them a family-tree diagram, the other a blank sheet of paper. The one with the diagram dictates the names and relationships, improvising sentences from the diagram using the possessive *'s* as above, so that the other can reconstruct it.

2 Each student dictates to his or her partner his or her own immediate family.

Box 15.3a: Family tree

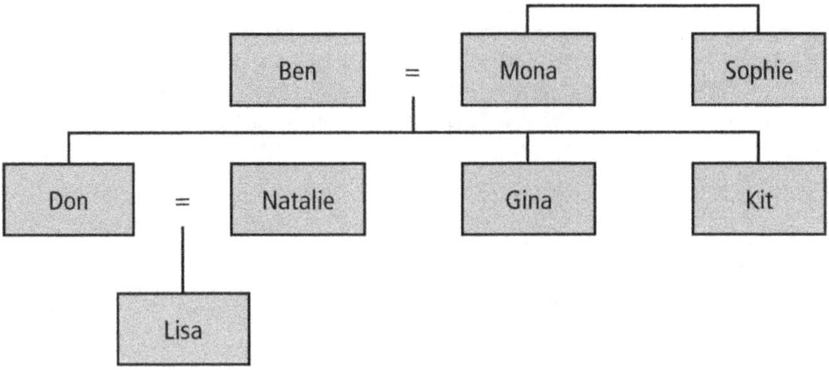

Box 15.3b: Family tree

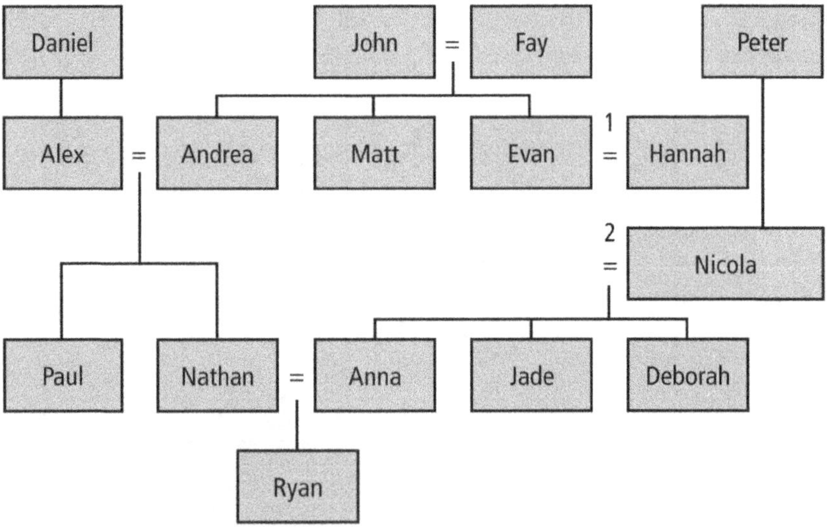

15.4 Whose is it?

Focus	*'s* or possessive determiners or pronouns to indicate possession
Age	Any
Level	Elementary–Intermediate
Time	20–25 minutes
Preparation	Ask each member of the class to give you one or two small objects belonging to them; each object should be in some way identifiable as belonging to its owner: a hair slide from someone with long hair, a sheet of music from someone who plays an instrument. Ask students the day before the lesson to bring the articles with them to class, but not to show them to anyone except you.

Procedure

1 Place the articles on a table in the middle of the room, and make sure that all the students know what they are called in English – if necessary, write up new words on the board.

2 Each student takes an article and notes down in writing whose it is (if he/she doesn't know – he/she should guess anyway). For example:

    The red hair slide is Talia's.

3 The student then returns the article to the table, and takes another. And so on, until most of the objects have been looked at two or three times, or until you feel the students have had enough.

4 Check answers, using and eliciting possessive pronouns. For example:

    Is this your hair slide? / Is this yours, Talia?
    No, it isn't mine. It's Anat's.

Who got the most right answers?

Variation

Instead of step 4, students check their answers with the owners. For example:

    Is this your hair slide, Talia?

If they find out they were wrong, they ask other students until they find out whose the object is.

Follow-up

Invite individual students to talk about their article and experiences connected with it.

Note

Make sure that at least four or five students do in fact bring two objects, so that there will always be a reserve of objects on the central table.

15.5 Distributing goods

Focus	Possessive determiners and pronouns (*our*, *their*, *ours*, *theirs*)
Age	Any
Level	Elementary–Intermediate
Time	15–20 minutes
Preparation	Piles of pictures of objects (see *Box 15.5*)

Procedure

1 Tell the class that the objects are available for use on one of two holidays: 'we' are going on an active outdoor holiday in a mountainous area, whereas 'they' (a rival class or school) are going on a restful, luxurious one on a hot tropical island (or vice versa!).

2 In groups, they have to decide which objects are 'ours' and which are 'theirs'. For example:

Is this our backpack or theirs?
Is this their walking stick or ours?
It's ours/theirs.

and put them into two piles according to their decision.

3 Note that some items, such as the camera, could belong to either group: if they can't decide which group it goes to, they can have a third pile: ours or theirs.

Variation

The same can be done with other possessives: if two holidaymakers have names, then the *'s* is used; if one is male and one is female (unnamed), then *his/her/his/hers;* if students are working in pairs, then each can take one of the roles, using *my/your/mine/yours*.

Box 15.5: Distributing goods

16 Prepositions

16.1 Where were you?

Focus	Prepositional phrases of time and place, and their order (place before time)
Age	Young–Teenager
Level	Beginner–Elementary
Time	10–15 minutes
Preparation	Tables (see *Boxes 16.1a* and *16.1b*) copied for students

Procedure

1 Each student gets the first table and circles an option in each of the three columns, indicating altogether an imaginary (or true!) personal situation at some time last week.

2 He/she tries to find other students who were at the same place at the same time, by asking simple questions based on the text of the table. For example:

Were you in town?
Were you in town at six o'clock?
Were you in town on Saturday?

3 They then do the same with the imaginary future situation shown in the second table.

Box 16.1a: Where were you?

1 I was ...		
... in town	at six o'clock (pm)	on Friday.
... at home	at one o'clock (pm)	on Wednesday.
... at school	at ten o'clock (am)	on Saturday.

Box 16.1b: Where were you?

2 I will be ...		
... in London	in February	for three days.
... in Rio de Janeiro	in June	for a week.
... in Bangkok	in December	for a month.

16.2 On the table

Focus Simple prepositions of place (*on*, *under*, *in*, *near*) to describe a scene
Age Young
Level Beginner–Elementary
Time 20–30 minutes
Preparation One set of pictures (see *Box 8.3a*), cut up into separate pictures (the 'complete' pictures), and a copy of the 'base' picture (see *Box 16.2*) for each student in the class

Procedure

1 Distribute the 'base' pictures to students. Explain that these need to be completed by drawing in various items.
2 List or draw these items on the board: an egg, an apple, a bird, a cat, a dog.
3 Now put the students in pairs, and give to one member of each pair one of the 'complete' pictures. The student with this complete picture may not display it to his/her partner, but explains where to draw in the items. For example:
  The egg is on the table.
  The cat is under the tree.
4 Tell students that they can draw very rough representations of the cat, dog, etc. These don't have to be exactly the same as the complete pictures, just in the right places!

5 When they finish, the two students compare their pictures to check that the new drawing is accurate.
6 They then exchange roles: the student who was previously drawing gets a 'complete' picture to describe to his/her partner, and the process is repeated.

Variations

1 The person drawing may of course request further information by asking:

> Where is the cat?
> Is the dog standing or sitting?

2 Using only the completed pictures from *Box 8.3a*, do a 'finding pairs' activity as described in *8.3 Find a twin picture*.

Box 16.2: On the table

16.3 In on at

Focus *In, on, at* referring to times
Age Any
Level Beginner–Elementary
Time 10–15 minutes

Procedure

1 Challenge students to brainstorm all the words or phrases denoting times that they can think of: one o'clock, Sunday, Christmas, the spring, 2010, January. Add some of your own if you feel they have neglected any types of times.

2 When you have at least 15 items on the board, challenge them to come to the board and insert *in, on, at* before the items.

Variations

1 Remind students before you start – or after you finish! – of the generalization about *in, on, at* with times: *in* is used with a lengthy time (a year, month, season); *on* is used with days or specific dates; *at* refers to a point in time (a festival or a time of day).

2 At step 2, students may stay where they are and just suggest which prepositions go where: you fill them in yourself.

Follow-up

Invite students to take two times, put them together, and then suggest an ending:

At six o'clock on Thursday there's a good programme on television.

Teaching tip

When getting students to write on the board, you don't have to limit it to one at a time; two or three students can be working simultaneously, which allows a lot more participation and a faster pace. Any student who finishes filling in one item hands his/her marker or chalk to another student to fill in another.

16.4 Guessing locations

Focus	Prepositions of place in 'yes/no' questions
Age	Young
Level	Beginner
Time	10–15 minutes
Preparation	Five or six small objects or toys representing things the students know how to say in English: a toy dog or car, for example, a little book or small food items

Procedure

1 Review names of classroom furniture and other items: *table, chair, board, door, window, shelf, cupboard, drawer.*

2 Tell the students to close their eyes.

3 Hide the items you have collected in various places round the classroom (students will of course hear where you are going as you do the hiding: but they will not know exactly which object you have put in each place).

4 Tell the students to open their eyes, and write up the names of (or draw) the items you have hidden on the board.

5 Challenge the students to guess where the items are. For example:

> Is the car near the board?
> Is it under a book?

6 Tell them how close they are by using phrases such as 'very close', 'close', 'far', 'very far'.

7 They may **not** get up and go and look until they have 'found' an item!

Variations

1 Hide the items before the students come to the class.

2 Without using actual objects, tell students you have in your imagination hidden a 'treasure' somewhere in the classroom / the school. They guess where it is.

16.5 Describe and arrange

Focus	Prepositions of place in instructions
Age	Young
Level	Beginner–Elementary
Time	15–25 minutes
Preparation	An identical set of toy building bricks or Cuisenaire rods of varied sizes and colours for each student

Procedure

1 Give students instructions how to arrange the components. For example:

Put the yellow rod across the black rod ...

Put the red brick behind the white brick ...

2 Then in pairs: one student arranges his or her materials in a pattern the other cannot see and then gives his/her partner instructions how to lay them out. At the end, they check they have the same pattern.

Variations

1 The student giving the instructions gets a sketch of the desired layout (see *Box 16.5a*), and dictates from that. Then the other student gets a sketch and the roles are reversed. If several copies of each sketch are made, they can be exchanged as they finish, until every pair of students has done as many as possible in the time.

2 The same can be done by printing out the colour version of the sketches from CD-ROM *Box 16.5b*.

Box 16.5a: Describe and arrange

1

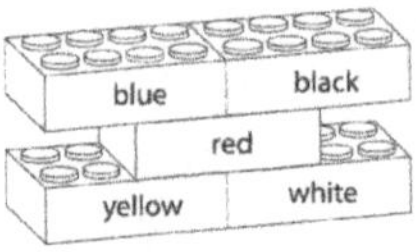

2

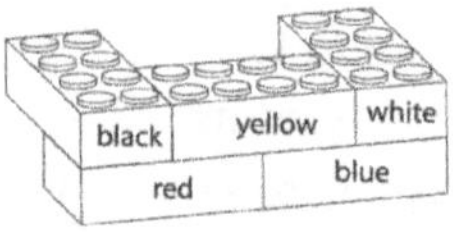

3

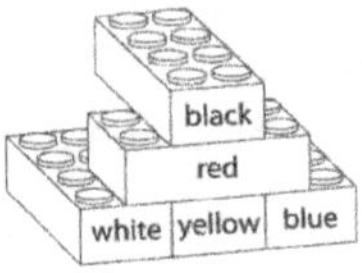

4

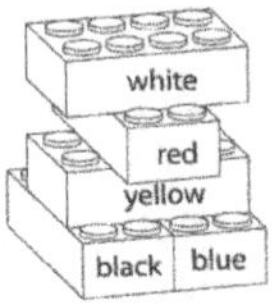

5

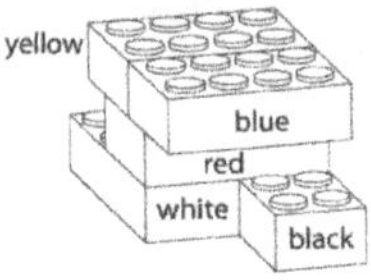

6

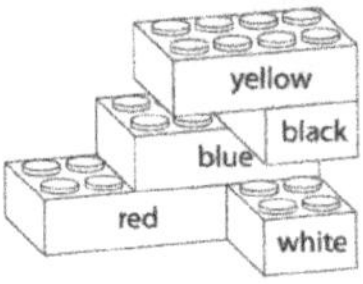

7

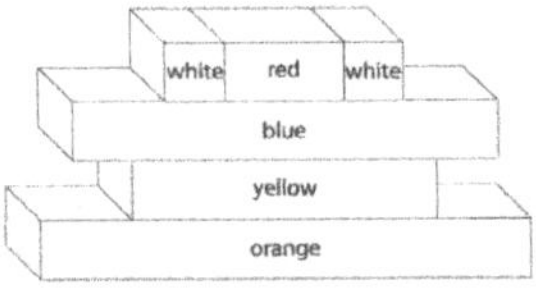

8

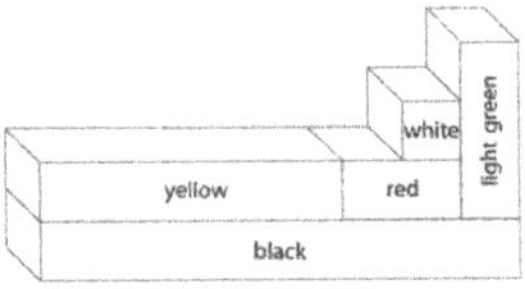

9

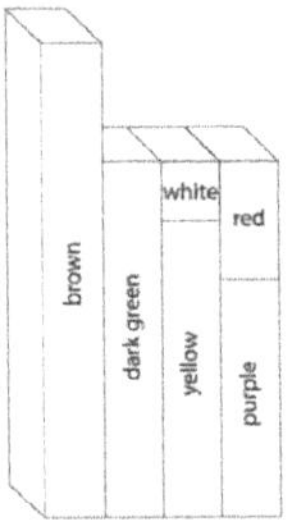

10

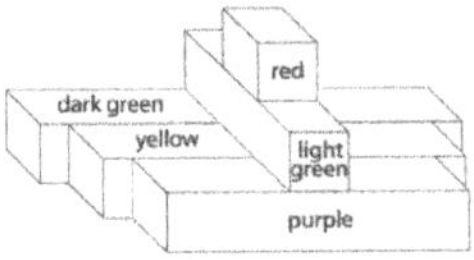

11

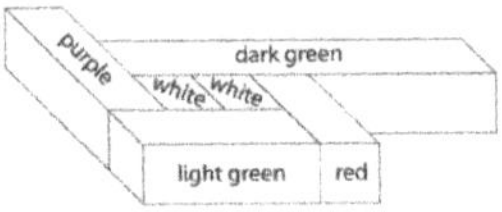

12

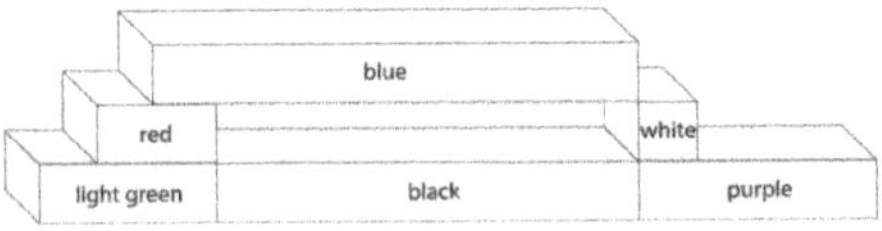

16.6 Where would you like to live?

Focus	Prepositions of place or direction to locate points on a map
Age	Any
Level	Elementary–Intermediate
Time	20–30 minutes
Preparation	A map of an urban or rural area shown on the board or copied for students. You could use the urban map in *Box 5.2* or one of the island maps in *Box 13.3a*, or a local map.

Procedure

1 Tell the students where you would like to live, if you could choose, in the area on the map. For example:

I'd like to live in the Nature Reserve, by the river, on the right bank.

2 Then ask each student to write down a description of where he or she would like to live; they must pinpoint the location by using at least three prepositional phrases. You might help by suggesting prepositions they could use: *near*, *by*, *on*, *in*, *under*, *opposite*, *beside*, *above*, *below*, *not far from*, *in the middle of*, *at the foot of*, *at the top of*, *at the end of*, etc.

3 Students mark on the map their chosen place to live.

4 Students ask each other where they'd like to live and mark in the other locations with the names of the students who have chosen to live there.

5 Ask a few students where they chose to live and why. Discuss: who lives near whom? What kinds of places do most students choose to live in? Why did people choose to live where they do?

Variation

Instead of describing the location, students can direct each other to their homes, starting from a clearly defined point determined by you. The prepositions then will be ones of direction and movement: *to*, *into*, *past*, *by*, *along*, *over*, *under*, *down*, *up*, *up to*, *as far as*, *across*, *through*, *via*, *beyond*, etc.

16.7 Preposition poem

Focus Prepositions of any kind
Age Any
Level Intermediate–Advanced
Time 20–30 minutes
Preparation A sample preposition poem (see *Box 16.7b*) shown on the board or copied for students; optionally, copies of the prepositions (see *Box 16.7a*)

Procedure

1 Brainstorm and write up on the board as many prepositions as the students can think of; or distribute copies of *Box 16.7a*.
2 Show the students the sample preposition poem.
3 Challenge them to write poems of their own. They should start by composing a final, preferably dramatic, event such as 'We fall in love' or 'They escaped from the enemy'. Then they think of all the circumstances (time, place or other) and add prepositional phrases that provide the circumstances or preceding events.
4 Students read out their poems to the class or write them out neatly and post them on the classroom wall or on a class website.

Variation

Students can work in pairs to compose their poems.

Box 16.7a: Preposition poem

Prepositions

Place (static): at, in, on, under, near, behind, in front of, above, among, around, below, beneath, beside, between, beyond, by, inside, outside, opposite, in the middle of, at the end of, at the top of, close to

Place (movement): to, into, out of, through, over, across, along, round, beyond, down, up, towards, past, as far as, via

Time: in, on, at, before, after, during, until, about

Other relationships: about, against, by, except, with, for, from, of, off, without, because of, in spite of

Box 16.7b: Preposition poem

Through the dark wet mists,
Beside the rushing river,
Into gigantic, beautiful trees,
Close to toucans and big, wet leaves,
We got lost in the rain forest.

Writing Simple Poems
Pairisblu Davis and Neydi Contreras

16.8 Who's she talking to?

Focus	Prepositions at the end of questions
Age	Teenager–Adult
Level	Intermediate–Advanced
Time	20–30 minutes
Preparation	A picture or two (see *Boxes 16.8a–d* for some examples) shown on the board or copied for students; copies of skeleton questions (see *Box 16.8e* for some examples) for students

Procedure

1 Show the picture, and invite students to compose at least six questions about the character shown in it. They must use at least four of the 'skeleton' questions shown in *Box 16.8e*, but may use other kinds of questions as well. For example:

Who's she talking to?
What's she looking at?
What's she frightened of?

2 The students ask you their questions: you give answers from your imagination, gradually building up the circumstances, until you have a whole situation.

3 Repeat some details about the character: can the students recall the question that was asked in order to elicit it?

LANGUAGE TIP

In formal English prose it is common to insert the preposition before the noun phrase it governs: 'To whom ... ' rather than 'Who ... to'; 'About which' rather than 'Which ... about'.

Box 16.8a: Who's she talking to?

Box 16.8b: Who's she talking to?

Box 16.8c: Who's she talking to?

Box 16.8d: Who's she talking to?

Box 16.8e: Who's she talking to?

Skeleton questions

Who/what/where ... to?

Who/what ... at?

Who/what ... with?

Who/what ... about?

Who/what/where ... from?

Who/what ... for?

Who/what ... on?

Who/what ... of?

17 Present tenses

17.1 PRESENT SIMPLE

17.1.1 Detectives

Focus	The present simple of *have*
Age	Young
Level	Beginner
Time	15–20 minutes

Procedure

1 An object to be 'stolen' is decided on – say a coin or a ring. One student (the 'detective') is sent out of the room. One of the remaining students is given the object: he or she is the 'thief'.

2 The detective returns and tries to find out who the thief is by asking each participant:

Do you have it / the ring?

Each participant – including the actual thief – denies guilt, and accuses someone else:

No, I don't have it. Alice (or Max, or he or she) has it!

3 The detective turns to Alice with the same question – and so on, until everyone has been asked and has denied responsibility.

4 The detective then has to decide in three guesses who is lying – who 'looks guilty'. The process is then repeated with another detective and another thief.

Note

This is a variation of *15.2 Who is lying?*

Variation

The activity may be made more lively by encouraging students to act innocence or indignation as convincingly as they can: they may change the emphasis or intonation of the set sentences as they wish, add gesture and so on.

> **Language tip**
>
> In British English the form *have got* is often used instead of *have* in the present simple. However, the straightforward form *have* is more common in American English and probably worldwide, and is much easier to teach (it also has regular past and future tenses!).

17.1.2 Possessions

Focus	Present simple of *have*
Age	Young
Level	Beginner–Elementary
Time	15–20 minutes
Preparation	Pictures of small objects whose names in the target language are known to the students (see *Box 11.3.1*)

Procedure

1 Each student gets a picture. Going round the class, each says what he or she has. For example:

I have a cat.
I have some coffee.
I have a box of matches.

2 Students are challenged to recall what others have. For example:

Ahmad has a cat.
Hasan has some coffee.
Fayiz has a box of matches.

Variations

1 Students say not only what they have but also what they don't have – and the latter, of course, is open to the individual student's imagination. For example:

I have a dog (*shows it*), but I don't have an elephant.
I have a fish, but I don't have a dolphin.

The recallers then have to remember not only what the other participants have, but also what they do not have – again, using the third person.

2 In a more personalized version, students don't use given pictures but imagine their own items, choosing things they really have that are 'special' for them. They may add brief comments about their 'possession'. (This is a good getting-to-know-you activity for an early stage in the course.)

17.1.3 Animal habits

Focus	Present simple to describe habitual action or general facts
Age	Young
Level	Elementary
Time	20–30 minutes

Procedure

1 Give the class the name of an animal, and ask them what they know about its habits. For example, a rabbit:

It lives in a hole.
It eats plants and vegetables.
It has a lot of babies.
It runs very fast.

2 If students can't think of anything to say, suggest verbs they might base their sentences on (*have, live, eat, move, sleep, make, change, grow, like, hate*).

3 Then ask them, in groups or pairs, to prepare a description of the habits of an animal of their choice.

4 Each group reads out its description to the rest of the class, who guess what the animal is.

Follow-up

For homework, ask the students to choose an animal and find out as much as they can about it, by looking it up in nature or zoology books or on the Internet. In a later lesson, invite them to give brief talks about the animals they have studied.

17.1.4 Opinion questionnaires

Focus	Present simple to describe states of feeling, thinking, etc.
Age	Teenager–Adult
Level	Elementary–Intermediate
Time	20–30 minutes
Preparation	Copies of questionnaires designed to elicit opinions on some subject of interest to the class; *Box 17.1.4* is a feedback sheet on the English course the students are currently doing, but you could construct similar questionnaires on any topic of general or local interest (other questionnaires that can be adapted for this activity can be found in *Boxes 2.2.1a, b; 7.1.3a, b; 10.4a–c; 21.2.2a–f*).

Procedure

1 Give out the questionnaires, and go through them if necessary to check that they are understood.

2 Ask students to work on their own, marking in their answers to each question.

3 When most have finished, they get into pairs and compare their answers. They should express these as full sentences, not just read out the chosen option. For example:

I find the material easy.
Well, I find it too difficult!

4 Finally, share ideas in the full class.

Follow-up

1 For homework, each student writes a summary of his or her opinion of the topic of the questionnaire, in essay form, using the questionnaire answers as a source of ideas.

2 Students may also be asked to design their own questionnaires, eliciting opinions of classmates on topics that interest them.

Teaching tip

In general, it's really helpful to get students to provide feedback like this on your course at regular intervals! Use this questionnaire, or ask them simply to write you letters telling you what things help / don't help them learn in the lessons.

Box 17.1.4: Opinion questionnaires

Feedback on this course

Please underline the appropriate answer.

1 **How much do you feel you have learnt on this course so far?**
a lot / quite a lot / not much / nothing

2 **Do you find the material:**
too easy? / too difficult? / about the right level of difficulty?

3 **How do you rate the teaching?**
excellent / good / all right / not very good / bad / terrible

4 **Do you think you get:**
too much homework? / too little homework? / about the right amount of homework?

5 **Do you consider the material interesting?**
yes, very / yes, quite / no, not very / no, it's very boring

6 **Do you want:**
more grammar? / more vocabulary work? / more listening? / more talking? / more reading? / more writing? / other? (say what)

____

____

7 **In general, do you prefer:**
working on your own? / working in pairs or small groups? / working in the full class? / being teacher-directed?

8 **Do you think you should have tests:**
once a week? / once a month? / less than once a month? / never?

9 **Do you like playing games in class?**
yes / sometimes / no

10 **Do you enjoy the English course, in general?**
yes, very much / yes / not very much / no, not at all

If you have any further comments, please write them below.

____

____

____

____

____

____

____

____

17.1.5 Routines

Focus	Present simple to describe routines
Age	Any
Level	Elementary–Intermediate
Time	25–30 minutes

Procedure

1 Discuss briefly activities we do as part of our daily routine, and ask for examples of things people do regularly once a week, once a month, once a year. For example:

I visit my grandmother once a month.
I take my vitamin pill once a day.

2 Give the students five minutes to write down as many things as they can think of that they do …

… every day
… about once a month
… about once a year.

3 They should write their suggestions in full sentences, like the examples above; supply new vocabulary as needed.

4 In groups, students read out their lists to one another and delete anything they have written down which someone else has as well. So that at the end, each student has only his or her 'special' routines that no one else has. Later, a representative from each group describes these 'special' routines in the third person. For example:

Justine goes to ballet class every day.
Paul doesn't eat anything for one day every month.

5 Some of these routines may give rise to interesting questions and answers – also in the present simple.

17.1.6 Guessing occupations

Focus	Present simple to describe habitual action: interrogatives and short answers
Age	Any
Level	Elementary
Time	20–30 minutes
Preparation	Slips of paper on each of which is written a name and an occupation (see *Box 17.1.6*)

Procedure

1. One student takes a slip, says the name of the person and gives a simple hint as to what the occupation is. For example:

   Her name is Dara. She works inside.

   His name is Andrew. He doesn't work at night.

   If the gender is not apparent from the name, the student may decide arbitrarily if it's a man or a woman.
2. Other students try to guess what the job is; they may ask general questions, in the present simple. For example:

   Does she work with other people?

   Does he wear a uniform?
3. They may only make three direct guesses as to the occupation ('Is she a cleaner?'), so should be very sure of their ground before doing so.

Variations

1. Students choose names and occupations on their own, rather than relying on given slips.
2. Students present the occupation as their own. So they begin 'I work outside', and other students ask them 'Do you ... ?'

Note

Remind students that in English we say Joshua is *an* actor; some languages don't have indefinite articles, others have them but don't use them when people are saying what someone's occupation is (French, for example); in any case, omitting the indefinite article here is a common learner mistake. See *11.1.3 Occupations* for further practice on this point.

Box 17.1.6: Guessing occupations

Megan a detective	Nancy a cleaner	Chris a mechanic
Lindsay a photographer	Jeff a street cleaner	Joshua an actor
Andrew a farmer	Dara a hairdresser	Evan a model
Janice a chef	Michael a photographer	Bonnie a bus driver
Daniel a pilot	Heidi a singer	Pete a computer programmer
Ross a poet	Fiona a dress designer	Emily a surgeon
Rachel a journalist	Elliot a waiter	Harry a flight attendant

Language tip

It's worth making the students aware that the present simple is easily the most common verb form in the English language: if they're not sure whether to use the present simple or present progressive in their own writing or speech, they should know that statistically the present simple is more likely to be the right choice!

17.1.7 What I do and don't do

Focus	Affirmative and negative of the present simple to describe habitual action or state
Age	Any
Level	Elementary–Intermediate
Time	20–30 minutes

Procedure

1 List on the board a number of fields of activity or habit, such as: sports, eating, leisure-time activity, entertainment, clothes, work, study – and any more the students can think of and add.

2 Ask students to choose any field they like and write one thing that they do and one thing that they don't do in that field (and don't mind telling other people about). If they finish, they should go on to another, and do the same again. They may add reasons or any other relevant detail. For example:

Sport: I watch tennis, but I don't play it.
Eating: I eat chicken, but I don't eat pork.

3 Then students get into small groups and tell each other about themselves.

4 Students tell the rest of the class about other people in their group. For example:

As'ad watches tennis, but doesn't play it ... he eats chicken but he doesn't eat pork ...

Note

This is a good activity for the beginning of the course, when students are getting to know one another.

17.1.8 Something special

Focus	Present simple to describe habitual action or state
Age	Any
Level	Elementary–Intermediate
Time	20–30 minutes

Procedure

1 Ask each student to think of, and perhaps write down, one interesting (present) fact about him- or herself (an unusual hobby, habit, characteristic, job, possession, etc.) that he or she would be willing to talk about – and do the same yourself. For example:

I go bird-watching every weekend.
I only eat natural foods.

2 Tell the students the special fact about yourself. Perhaps answer questions or elaborate a little.

3 Invite students to share their 'special things', answer questions and discuss them.

Variation

Students can write full paragraphs about their topics and present them later in class.

Note

Again, a good getting-to-know-you activity.

17.1.9 What do you feel about it?

Focus	Present simple to describe feeling or opinion
Age	Any
Level	Elementary–Intermediate
Time	25–30 minutes
Preparation	A pile of coloured photographs depicting objects, animals, scenes, etc., cut out from magazines or downloaded from the Internet

Procedure

1 Spread the pictures on a table in the middle of the classroom, and invite each student to choose one that arouses some kind of definite positive or negative reaction in him or her. Choose one for yourself.

2 Then invite each to show his or her picture and say whether he or she likes it or not, and why. Start the ball rolling yourself with a comment on the picture you have chosen.

   I love this picture. The colours make me feel relaxed ...

Note

Not all the student responses will be in the present simple; they may respond to a picture because it reminds them of something that happened in the past, or something they hope will happen in the future. This is acceptable; the main thing is that the students' descriptions of their own reactions ('I think/feel/like/hate ...') should be in the present simple.

17.1.10 Things in common

Focus	Present simple to describe habitual action or state
Age	Any
Level	Elementary–Intermediate
Time	15–25 minutes

Procedure

1 Students work in pairs: their partner should be someone they do not know very well.

2 The partners talk to each other and try to find as many things as they can in common with one another in three minutes. These should not include things they can find out just by looking at one another, e.g. that they both have blue eyes or are wearing jeans; nor should they include more than two things beginning 'We both like ...'.

3 Optionally, suggest some things they might talk about: things they like or don't like, things they do regularly, possessions, family; and remind them that all the things they find need to relate to the present.

4 Students should write down the things they find out they have in common in full sentences. For example:

   We both have two brothers.
   We both like reading detective stories.

5 Then ask the pairs to describe their common features.

Notes

1 Draw students' attention to the fact that if they use *be* in their sentences, then *both* comes after the verb: 'We are both married'.

2 Another good getting-to-know-you activity.

Variations

1 If you want to make sure that the third person form (problematical for a lot of learners) is practised, then tell the students to use sentences like: 'Talma has two brothers; so do I', or 'Talma is married; so am I'. This also gives practice in the forms 'so do I', 'so am I'.

2 Each student has to find at least one thing in common with as many other members of the class as they can; each talks to a partner for as long as necessary to discover a common feature, then changes partners. They note down names and common features as they find them. At the end, call out pairs of names at random, and find out what the two students have in common.

17.1.11 Changing proverbs

Focus	Present simple to express general truths
Age	Teenager–Adult
Level	Intermediate–Advanced
Time	20–30 minutes
Preparation	A list of well-known proverbs using the present simple (see *Box 17.1.11* for some examples) shown on the board or copied for students

Procedure

1 With the class, work through the list of proverbs you have selected, clarifying any difficult vocabulary and making sure their meanings are understood.

2 Divide the class into small groups, and ask each group to pick out proverbs they think are misleading or would like to change, discuss what is wrong with them and invent a version that seems to them to be preferable.

3 At the end, come together and discuss each proverb and its new versions.

Variations

1 Students can be asked to learn the proverbs by heart; then ask them to recall and write out as many as they can.

2 It is quite interesting to compare parallel proverbs in the students' own language(s), and discuss differences/similarities.

Box 17.1.11: Changing proverbs

- A bad workman blames his tools.
- A new broom sweeps clean.
- A stitch in time saves nine.
- Absence makes the heart grow fonder.
- Actions speak louder than words.
- All good things come to an end.
- All things come to him who waits.
- Bad news travels fast.
- Dreams go by contraries.
- Eavesdroppers hear no good of themselves.
- Every cloud has a silver lining.
- Every man has his price.
- Familiarity breeds contempt.
- Fine feathers make fine birds.
- God helps them that help themselves.
- Good fences make good neighbours.
- Great minds think alike.
- He who laughs last laughs best.
- History repeats itself.
- Love makes the world go round.
- Many hands make light work.
- Nothing succeeds like success.
- Practice makes perfect.
- Pride comes before a fall.
- Still waters run deep.
- The early bird catches the worm.
- The more you have, the more you want.
- Too many cooks spoil the broth.
- Two wrongs don't make a right.
- With age comes wisdom.

17.1.12 Is it true?

Focus	Present simple to describe facts; interrogatives and short answers
Age	Any
Level	Elementary–Intermediate
Time	15–20 minutes

Procedure

1 Write on the board three sentences about yourself in the present simple: two should be true and one false.
2 Invite students to ask you questions about the three statements; answer these questions.
3 After five minutes or so of question and answer, challenge students to guess which statements were true and which was false.
4 Students write three similar statements for themselves.
5 One of the students writes his/her statements on the board, and the same procedure as steps 2–3 above is repeated.
6 Go on to do the same with other students, perhaps in a following lesson.

Teaching tip

Once students have learnt how to do a particular activity it's very easy to pick it up and continue in a following, or later, lesson. Classes quickly develop 'favourites': if an activity becomes a favourite, use it later as a 'filler' or to finish off a lesson.

17.1.13 Recall the plot

Focus	Present simple to recount the plot of a book, film, etc.
Age	Any
Level	Intermediate–Advanced
Time	15–20 minutes

Procedure

1 Tell the students about a film you have seen or a book you have read recently: recount the plot briefly, in the present simple.
2 Invite one or two of the students to do the same.

Follow-up

Have a 'May I recommend?' session in class: students recommend to one another films, books or plays, recounting parts of their plots. They may improvise their recommendations orally or read out a prepared written text.

17.1.14 Theme music

Focus	Present simple to recount the plot of a book, film, etc.
Age	Any
Level	Intermediate–Advanced
Time	15–20 minutes
Preparation	A recording of an evocative piece of instrumental music

Procedure

1 Play the class a recording of music, and tell them this is the soundtrack to a film. Can they imagine what kind of film it is and what sort of plot it has?

2 Students need not write down an entire story but should note down some details of a plot that seems to them to fit the music. For example:

> This must be a romantic film ... it's about a girl who falls in love with a handsome nobleman ...

17.2 PRESENT PROGRESSIVE

17.2.1 He is running too!

Focus	Present progressive verbs with third-person pronouns
Age	Young
Level	Beginner–Elementary
Time	20–25 minutes
Preparation	Copy the sets of pictures shown in *Box 17.2.1* and cut up into separate pictures. There should be enough copies so that each group of students will have two copies of every picture.

Procedure

1 Students work in small groups of not more than four participants. Each group's sets of pictures are randomly distributed before them, face down.

2 The first participant turns over any two cards and describes the pictures in brief present progressive sentences. For example:

He is running.
She is eating.

Then he/she replaces them face down.

3 This process is repeated, in turn, by the participants, the aim being to remember where the different cards were located and to turn up a matching pair ('He is running too!') – which then becomes the property of the one who found them.

4 The winner is the one who has the most pairs at the end.

Note

The same procedure is used in *11.2.1 Remembering pairs* to practise *a/an/some*.

17.2.2 What's going on?

Focus	Present progressive to describe action-in-progress
Age	Any
Level	Beginner–Elementary
Time	5–10 minutes
Preparation	A picture showing a lot of things going on: a street scene, for example, or a market (see *Boxes 14.2.2a, 14.2.2b* and *14.2.2c*) shown on the board or copied for students

Procedure

1 Ask students to brainstorm all the things that they can see going on in the picture; challenge them to make at least 20 different sentences. For example:

The woman is drinking tea.
The police officer is talking to the driver.

The sentences don't all have to be in the present progressive, but most of them naturally will be.

2 For each sentence they find, write a ✓ on the board, until you reach 20. If this is too easy, raise the target to 30!

Variations

1 Ask students to write down all the sentences they can think of to describe what's going on in the picture: they have four minutes to do this. Then share ideas orally in the full class as described above.

Box 17.2.1: He is running too!

2 Show the picture for a minute or so, then hide it and ask students to write down all the things that they can remember are going on. Check against the picture. The same can be done as a group competition: which group has remembered the most activities?

Language tip

The present progressive is an easy verb form to demonstrate in class, and perhaps for that reason is sometimes over-emphasized in courses: it is in fact a fairly rare form, in both speech and writing. Some students tend to overuse it in contexts where the present simple would be more appropriate (see *Language tip*, p. 261).

17.2.3 Guessing mimes

Focus	Present progressive questions in the second person
Age	Young–Teenager
Level	Beginner–Elementary
Time	15–20 minutes
Preparation	Slips of paper showing simple sentences in the present progressive (see *Boxes 17.2.3a and 17.2.3b*)

Procedure

1 One student is given a slip and mimes its content.
2 The other students try to guess what he/she is doing. For example:
   Are you holding something?
   Are you opening something?
3 The successful guesser is given the next slip.

Note

Notice that the items shown in *Boxes 17.2.3a* and *17.2.3b* all have objects as well as verbs. This is to make sure that the guessing process does not finish too quickly. It isn't enough to guess, for example 'Are you eating?': the students have to continue with questions beginning 'Are you eating a ...?' and so on.

Variation

Students think up their own activities to be guessed.

Box 17.2.3a: Guessing mimes

Mimes

You are opening a tin can.

You are making a cup of coffee.

You are watching a comedy on television.

You are writing an email.

You are trying to catch a mosquito.

You are reading a very sad story.

You are playing chess.

You are waiting for a train.

You are eating a sandwich.

You are talking to yourself.

Box 17.2.3b: Guessing mimes

Mimes

You are crossing a road.

You are listening to a pop song.

You are studying something difficult.

You are making a salad.

You are sending a text message on your mobile phone.

You are running a marathon.

You are picking apples.

You are climbing a mountain.

You are playing drums.

You are cleaning a window.

17.2.4 Silhouettes

Focus	Present progressive to describe action-in-progress, mainly in the interrogative
Age	Any
Level	Elementary–Intermediate
Time	10–20 minutes
Preparation	Outline shapes of people doing things (see *Box 17.2.4a*) which can be projected on the board, or simply cut out and displayed on a contrasting background. See *Note* for a do-it-yourself alternative.

Procedure

1 Display a silhouette on the board, or distribute copies to students.

2 Invite students to guess what sort of a person it is and what they are doing. They should use 'yes/no' questions. For example:

   Is it a man?

   Is he holding a musical instrument?

3 Answer their questions, adding further hints if you feel it necessary.

4 When they have guessed, reveal the original picture, and then proceed to another.

Note

An alternative is to cut out suitable silhouettes from glossy magazines or the pictures in *Box 17.2.4b* on the CD-ROM, and back them with dark-coloured card (if you are using a whiteboard) or light-coloured (if you are using a blackboard). Then stick them up on the board with the blank side showing, and simply turn them round to reveal the picture once they are guessed. This is very easy to adapt for the *Variation* below, and makes a nice impact when you turn round the picture.

Variation

You can put up several silhouettes at once, numbering them, and ask students to guess whichever one they like. This means that when they despair of, or get fed up with, one of them, they can move on to one of the others. This tends to make for a faster-paced and more interesting process.

Box 17.2.4a: Silhouettes

1

2

3

4

5

6

Box 17.2.4b: Silhouettes

1

2

3

4

5

6

17.2.5 Temporary and permanent

Focus	Present progressive contrasted with present simple to express temporary and permanent states
Age	Any
Level	Elementary–Intermediate
Time	15–20 minutes

Procedure

1 Describe to the class some things you are doing temporarily, and contrast with more permanent or usual situations. For example:

At the moment I'm speaking English, but most of the time I speak French.

This year I'm living in Seoul, but my permanent home is in Scotland.

2 Ask the students to write down a few similar sentences. They may begin them with:

At the moment ...

Today ...

This year/month/week ...

3 Students read out their sentences.

4 Encourage other students to ask questions. For example:

Are you enjoying living in Paris?

Where do you live in Scotland?

Variations

1 Tell students to read out only one half of their sentence. For example:

At the moment I'm not feeling very well ...

or:

I usually use a computer ...

and ask others to try to reconstruct what the other half is. The one whose guess is nearest to the original suggests the next half-sentence.

2 Invite students to relate to people they know rather than themselves.

18 Pronouns

18.1 Reverse guessing (2)

Focus	Subject and object pronouns; possessive determiners
Age	Any
Level	Beginner–Elementary
Time	15–20 minutes

Procedure

1 One student is sent out of the room, and the rest of the class chooses an object or person to be guessed.

2 When the student comes back, he or she is told if the item to be guessed is *he, she* or *it*, and whether it is singular or plural.

3 Students in the class then suggest hint after hint as to what the item is, using the appropriate pronouns, until the student is enabled to guess the answer. For example, if the answer is (the name of) a well-known footballer, the class may say things like:

He is a man.
His picture is on football posters.
We see him on television.

4 The guesser should not guess, even if he or she is fairly sure of the answer, until the rest of the class has exhausted their ideas for hints.

Variations

1 In order to practise the plural pronouns, tell the students to choose names of objects, animals or people, expressed in the plural: *telephones, kangaroos* or *mothers*, for example.

2 First-person plurals can be elicited if the class identify with the objects to be guessed: 'Guess who we are! You eat us! We grow on trees!', etc.

Follow-up

For a written assignment to follow, students can be asked to compose a series of hints in the form of simple sentences intended to lead to a certain solution. If this is done for homework, you then have not only to correct the grammar of the sentences, but also to guess the solutions. If done in class, the sets of sentences can be exchanged between students for guessing.

18.2 It's automatic!

Focus	Reflexive pronouns to indicate reflexive or independent action
Age	Any
Level	Intermediate–Advanced
Time	25–40 minutes
Preparation	Sample advertisements (see *Boxes 18.2a, 18.2b* and *18.2c*) shown on the board or copied for students

Procedure

1 Discuss the meaning of the word *automatic* as implying the quality, usually of equipment or machines, of being able to do things (to) themselves, without external agency.

2 Show the students the three advertisements, make sure they are understood, and discuss how possible they are. The first is entirely possible, the others are (at the time of writing!) imaginary and futuristic. Draw students' attention to the phrase *by –self*, as used in the third advertisement, meaning 'alone', or 'without help'.

3 Challenge students to write their own advertisements for male/female robots of various kinds, equipment or other facilities. If they have difficulty thinking of ideas, verbs given in *Box 18.2.d* may help.

Note

Remind students that either the simple reflexive form may be used (with transitive verbs) or the expression *by –self*.

Box 18.2.a: It's automatic!

ENGLISH COURSE

Teach yourself English!

Do our course and you will be able to teach yourself, give yourself practice and assess yourself using our tests.

Box 18.2.b: It's automatic!

AUTOMATIC LAWN!

A wonderful invention!

You don't need to do anything: just lay the lawn and let it look after itself. It will water itself, weed itself and cut itself regularly.

Box 18.2.c: It's automatic!

Electric robot housecleaner

She's wonderful! She's automatic!

She cleans and tidies the house by herself. She cleans herself too and recharges herself regularly.

Box 18.2.d: It's automatic!

wash	sweep	write
cook	teach	come back
talk to	go	prepare
fill	close	look after
open	clean	empty
cut	take care of	pay

18.3 Who are they?

Focus	Pronouns of various kinds
Age	Any
Level	Intermediate
Time	30–40 minutes
Preparation	Short dialogues shown on the board or copied for students. These should use a lot of pronouns and possessive determiners, but have no antecedents, so the context is unclear (see *Box 18.3* for some examples).

Procedure

1 Display one of the dialogues on the board, or provide each student with a copy, and challenge them to work out who is speaking and what it's about.

2 Make sure they tell you specifically who is meant by each of the personal pronouns mentioned.

3 Discuss the various possibilities: there is no one right answer, but the class should be able to think up at least four or five different ideas.

4 Students work in pairs on the next dialogue and add at least three or four further lines that fit their interpretation.

5 Invite some or all of the pairs to explain the circumstances of their dialogue and who the pronouns represent – and to act out their finished dialogues.

Note

This activity covers a wider range of pronominal forms than the previous one, and provides opportunities for you to teach or review the expression *by –self* or the use of the reflexive pronoun for emphasis, to draw attention to some commonly confused forms (*her* and *hers*, for example), or focus on common errors (*themselves*, not **theirself*, for example).

Variations

1 Instead of explaining the interpretation, the pairs simply act out their dialogues, trying to make their interpretation as clear as possible through intonation, gesture, etc. The rest of the class then tries to guess the characters and interpretations.

2 Students compose their own similar dialogues and act them out, challenging the rest of the class to interpret them.

Box 18.3: Who are they?

Dialogue 1

A: She told him, you know.

B: No! She didn't!

A: Yes. What do you think he'll do?

B: He can't manage by himself, anyhow. He needs our help.

A: Ours, and theirs too.

Dialogue 2

A: Whose are they?

B: I don't know. Not mine – and not hers either.

A: But they're in your car.

B: It's not our car, it's his. Maybe they're his.
Why don't you ask him?

A: We will.

Dialogue 3

A: You really ought to talk to her yourself.

B: Me? I can't. She won't listen to me.

A: Well, then maybe I can try myself.

B: Good idea. After all, you're the one who found her.

Dialogue 4

A: Pick them up!

B: OK, OK. Here they are.

A: Which do you think is nicer?

B: This one. Or maybe that one. I don't know.

A. OK, we'll take them both.

18.4 Yourselves or each other?

Focus	The reflexive pronoun contrasted with the reciprocal *each other*
Age	Any
Level	Intermediate–Advanced
Time	20–25 minutes
Preparation	Make copies of a list of verbs or adjectives that could be used reflexively or reciprocally (e.g. talk to yourself / to each other) (see *Box 18.4*), so that there are enough to give one to each pair of students.

Procedure

1 Put students into pairs: each pair has a copy of the list of verbs.
2 Tell them they should prepare a brief 'act' (like a mime, except that you're allowed to talk!), which may show either a reflexive action ('We are … ourselves') or a reciprocal ('We are … each other'). They may use the verbs shown on the list or others they have thought up themselves.
3 Each pair in turn does their act: the rest of the class has to say what they are doing. For example:

    Vita and Sasha are talking to themselves.

  or:

    You are angry with each other.

Variation

Put the students into pairs and simply dictate what they are to do: 'Talk to each other!' or 'Talk to yourselves'. All the students respond simultaneously. Or ask one of the students to be the one to dictate the actions: they are not, of course, limited to the verbs in the list shown in *Box 18.4*.

Box 18.4: Yourselves or each other?

look at	laugh at	feed
listen to	whisper to	put … to sleep
talk to	congratulate	be pleased with
point at	draw	be sorry for
read to	blame	be angry with
write to	ask	sing to

19 Relative clauses

19.1 Likes and dislikes

Focus	Relative clauses to express preferences
Age	Any
Level	Intermediate–Advanced
Time	15–20 minutes

Procedure

1 Give the class the introductory cues:

I like people who ...

I dislike people who ...

and ask everyone to complete the sentences in writing according to their own opinions and preferences.

2 Ask students to tell you what they have written, and write up as many as you can of the results on the board: you then have a profile of the class's favourite – and un-favourite – kinds of people!

Variations

1 Give the students similar beginnings, but with different nouns, using a variety of types of relative clauses: 'days when ... ', 'places where ... ', 'teachers who ... ', 'films which ... ', 'lessons in which ... '.

2 Make the activity more dramatic by substituting 'love' and 'hate' for 'like' and 'dislike'.

3 Instead of pooling the students' sentences in the full class they can do the same in groups; or each student can go round trying to find someone else with the same likes and dislikes as him- or herself.

19.2 Relative quizzes

Focus	Relative clauses to provide definitions of nouns
Age	Any
Level	Intermediate–Advanced
Time	25–35 minutes
Preparation	A number of lists of different nouns known to the students; all the nouns on any one list begin with the same letter (see *Box 19.2*). Make one copy and cut it up so that each list is on a separate piece of paper.

Procedure

1 Write up one list on the board (the one beginning with *p*, for example), and ask students to suggest definitions for each item, using relative clauses. For example:

a police officer: Someone who catches criminals
a post office: A place where you can buy stamps
a pear: A fruit that grows on trees.
a pen: A thing you write with.

2 Write up the definitions on the board.

3 Divide the class into pairs or small groups, and give each of these one of the lists you have prepared (but not, of course, the one you have used for your initial demonstration). Ask them to make up a definition for each noun, based on the models provided on the board.

4 They should write out these definitions on a piece of paper, **without** the original nouns.

5 Go round checking their lists to make sure that the grammar is correct.

6 Groups exchange lists and try to guess what the nouns are that are being defined. Point out that all the nouns on any one list begin with the same letter. Once they have guessed two or three nouns, it will become clear what their shared initial letter is, which will help them guess the rest.

7 If there are any definitions that groups can't guess, they may, of course, ask the authors of the definitions what the answer is.

Language tip

Perhaps remind students about the possibility of omitting the relative pronoun when it is the object of the relative clause: 'a pear is a thing that/which you eat', or 'a thing you eat'. Also perhaps draw their attention to the use of the preposition at the end of the clause: 'a pen is a thing (that/which) you write with'.

Notes

1 The use of the same initial letter for the items in each list is helpful because it enables students to write easier and more general definitions for some of the nouns than otherwise would be necessary. They are also easier to guess: more 'success-oriented'.

2 You might prefer to spread this activity over two sessions; this gives you time to take in the lists of definitions and check and correct them before giving them out to be guessed.

Variations

1 Read out some of the sets of definitions in full class for everyone to guess together. The authors of the definitions, may not, of course, 'guess'.

2 You may ask the students themselves to compose the original list of nouns, instead of giving it to them ready-made.

Teaching tip

In any group-, pair- or individual work in class that involves writing, it is a good idea to spend the writing time moving around the classroom checking that the grammar and spelling are acceptable, and correcting where necessary.

Box 19.2: Relative quizzes

List 1
an alligator
air
August
an airport
apples
an African
Australia
an artist

List 2
a birthday
a baby
a book
Bangladesh
bottles
bread
a bus
a bedroom

List 3
a chair
Canada
a chicken
a cinema
coffee
Christmas
a cow
a carpenter

List 4
doors
a daughter
December
daytime
a doctor
a dream
Denmark
a duck

List 5
eyes
eight
an elephant
an engine
economics
England
the evening
an emperor

List 6
a hotel
hands
Hollywood
happiness
a helicopter
a hairdresser
history
a horse

List 7
milk
Malaysia
money
the morning
a map
a mother
matches
a motorbike

List 8
New Zealand
a newspaper
a neighbour
a nose
the news
night
a nurse
names

List 9
a pen
a panda
a police officer
a parrot
a pear
Poland
a post office
pain

List 10
a snake
a scientist
shoes
the summer
a shop
spaghetti
the sun
Saudi Arabia

List 11
tigers
a television
Thailand
time
a tomato
tennis
a tooth
a taxi driver

List 12
walls
work
water
the west
a wife
the winter
a waiter
Wales

19.3 Write your own test

Focus	Relative clauses to provide definitions of nouns and adjectives
Age	Any
Level	Intermediate–Advanced
Time	25–35 minutes
Preparation	A list of nouns, noun phrases or adjectives that the class has learnt recently

Procedure

1 Tell the students they are going to write their own vocabulary tests, which will be administered next lesson.

2 Give them the list of vocabulary, and ask each student (or each pair of students) to write a definition of at least ten of the items, using relative clauses. Beside each definition they leave a line where the answer will be filled in. For example:

An area where there is very little rain: ____________

3 With adjectives, they write a definition of a noun described by the adjective, and then put the noun beside the line. For example:

A man who has never learnt very much: An ___________ man.

4 Students then exchange and do each other's tests.

Variations

1 You can take in students' suggestions after the first session for checking and correcting, then administer the tests next time.

2 Take in the students' suggestions, and then compose a general class test using items composed by the students.

3 Suggest to the students that they make the list of items to be tested into a crossword puzzle, using websites such as www.puzzlemaker.com, and then use relative clauses to compose the clues to each item in the crossword.

Note

You might need to remind students of some of the more tricky forms of relative clauses: see *Language tips* pp. 285 and below.

> **Language tip**
>
> The formal *whom* as the object form of *who* is not usually used in speech; however, it may be used in formal writing, and may be preferred by some examiners in advanced examinations.

19.4 Extending a story

Focus	Non-defining relative clauses to provide extra information
Age	Any
Level	Intermediate–Advanced
Time	25–30 minutes
Preparation	A short story or anecdote. Retype the story (or write it on the board), leaving a comma and half-line gap and another comma after some of the nouns (see *Boxes 19.4a* and *19.4b* for some examples). Make a copy for each pair of students.

Procedure

1 Give each pair of students a copy of the story, and ask them to invent and write in relative clauses. For example:

... Jack, who was ten years old, ...

or:

... Jack, who loved working in his garden, ...

2 Elicit suggestions and choose one for each space.

3 If you have the story projected or ready-written on the board, fill in the suggestion you (or the students) like best in each case.

4 Finally, read out the finished story.

Notes

1 Remind students that you can't use the zero relative pronoun or the relative pronoun 'that' in this kind of clause (non-defining): they have to use *who* (or *whom*) and *which*.

2 Students might find it difficult to think of ideas for all the spaces: tell them that they don't have to fill in them all, they should start by filling the ones they can easily think of ideas for. If there is time, they can try to deal with the others later.

Teaching tip

In a task where there are a number of different items to deal with, it's a good idea to tell students to look first for the easy ones and do them, coming back to the more difficult ones later. This is also, of course, a good test-taking strategy!

Box 19.4a: Extending a story

Once there was a boy called Jack, ______________________________.
Jack lived with his mother, ______________________________, and they were very poor. One day his mother said to Jack, ______________________________:
'Go and sell our old cow, ______________________________, at the market.'
Jack set out, but on the way he met an old man, ______________________________.
The man said to Jack: 'Look at these beautiful beans, ______________________________
______________________________. Give me your cow, ______________________________
______________________________, and I'll give you these beans,
______________________________!' Jack gave the man his cow and took the beans and went back to his mother, ______________________________

Box 19.4b: Extending a story

A big black crow, ______________________________, was sitting in a tree with a big piece of cheese, ______________________________.
A fox, ______________________________, passed by and saw her.
'Oh crow!' said the fox, ______________________________, 'How beautiful you are! I'm sure you have a beautiful voice too! Please sing for me!'
The crow, ______________________________, opened her beak and sang.
The cheese, ______________________________, fell to the ground. The fox, ______________________________, took the cheese and ran off to share it with his wife, ______________________________, and children, ______________________________.

19.5 Things I want to complain about

Focus	Relative clauses that end in (or begin with) prepositions
Age	Any
Level	Intermediate–Advanced
Time	25–30 minutes

Procedure

1 Tell the students they (and you!) are going to have a complaining session – let off steam about all the things that bother them. But first they have to think of things to complain about; and these must be expressed by nouns with relative clauses that use prepositions. For example, they might like to complain about:

A person I work with
The house/town I live in
The book we learn from
The person I sat next to on the bus today

2 Get the students to brainstorm as many such phrases as they can think of. Write them on the board as they are suggested. You might help them by suggesting topics: people, surroundings, equipment, entertainment.

3 Now tell them to let loose their complaints! They can, of course, add to, modify or present variations of each other's suggestions.

The person I work with is always late for meetings ...
The classroom we usually study in is too cold: why can't they turn up the heating?

Note

It is up to you, of course, what exact forms you wish the relative clauses to take: you might wish to include the relative pronouns. For example:

The book which we learn from
The person who I sat next to

Or you might wish to use more formal phrasing, putting the preposition at the beginning of the relative clause. For example:

The people with whom I work
The house in which I live

In any case, make it clear through your own first examples what pattern(s) you wish your students to follow.

Variations

1 After the brainstorm, you might give students a few minutes to write down some complaints before sharing them orally.
2 Invite students to relate to things they are **pleased** about instead of complaints.

Follow-up

1 Discuss what might be done about the various problems. Invite students to offer each other friendly advice.
2 For homework, ask students to recall and write down things they and other people complained or were pleased about.

20 Short answers and tag questions

20.1 SHORT ANSWERS

20.1.1 Answering guesses

Focus	Short answers to 'yes/no' questions
Age	Any
Level	Beginner–Elementary
Time	15–20 minutes

Procedure

1 Divide the class into two teams (A and B), each of which chooses three items: one person, one object, one group of things or people.

2 The first team chooses one of their items to start with, and tells the second whether the item is represented by *he*, *she*, *it* or *they*.

3 Then anyone in the second team may ask 'yes/no' questions to elicit information, and anyone in the first team may reply – but the responses must include 'short answers', not just 'yes' or 'no'. For example:
Is it in this room? Yes, it is.
Does he work with a computer? Yes, he does.
Do we eat them? No, we don't.

4 Teams go on guessing each other's items until all have been discovered (if they are difficult to guess, suggest that the team gives a hint).

Note

Of course, almost any guessing game can be used to practise giving short answers: see *7.1.1 Guessing* and its *Variations*.

20.1.2 They do!

Focus	Short answers to 'yes/no' questions (without using *yes* or *no*)
Age	Any
Level	Elementary–Intermediate
Time	15–20 minutes
Preparation	A set of simple 'yes/no' questions with obvious answers (see *Box 20.1.2* for some examples, but it's good to supplement these with your own)

Procedure

1 Write on the board two columns, one headed 'Teacher' and one headed 'Students'.

2 Explain that you are going to try to get them to say 'yes' or 'no'. Every time you succeed in getting someone to say 'yes' or 'no', you get a point. Every time a student succeeds in giving a correct response using a short answer without 'yes' or 'no', the student gets a point. No answer at all, or a wrong answer, means a point to you! The side which reaches ten points first wins.

3 Ask a 'yes/no' question to which the answer is obvious. For example:

Do dogs have four legs?

4 Students raise their hands to suggest answers. The answer must *not* include the words 'yes' or 'no' but should consist only of a short answer. For example:

They do.

5 Make sure that as many different students as possible participate: it may be useful to have a rule that any individual student may only answer twice.

Variations

1 If the students are very good at this, raise the number of points that the winning side needs to get, and introduce a time-limit rule: the answer has to be given within five seconds.

2 The same can be done as a competition between two teams. The teams take turns asking and answering questions.

Notes

1 This is similar to the activity *7.1.4 Don't say yes or no,* but designed so that the main focus is on practising short answers rather than questions.

2 Note that the questions are purposely designed to have obvious answers: the challenge is not to supply previously unknown information, but to express that information in a way that is limited by 'rule' constraints. The activity is thus transformed into a 'game' (see *Introduction*, p. 17). Humour can be added by including the occasional absurd question ('Are oranges blue?' 'Does a bus driver drive a taxi?').

Box 20.1.2: They do!

- Do dogs have four legs?
- Do elephants have short noses?
- Do fish live in the sea?
- Is it 12 o'clock?
- Are you studying English?
- Can a duck run fast?
- Am I a mouse?
- Am I a woman?
- Do you know Chinese?
- Does a bus driver drive a taxi?
- Can a helicopter swim?
- Do you live in Norway?
- Does January come before February?
- Are there 70 minutes in an hour?
- Can you play the guitar?
- Is it Sunday today?
- Does a tiger eat meat?
- Is it cold in summer?
- Does a rich man have a lot of money?
- Are babies small?
- Does tea grow in Antarctica?
- Do you like chocolate ice cream?
- Are oranges blue?
- Can cows produce milk?
- Is the sun shining?
- Does money grow on trees?
- Can potatoes talk?
- Are you a boy?
- Are lemons sweet?
- Do we get information from the Internet?

Language tip

Draw your students' attention to the fact that when short answers are used instead of 'No' as a negative response, contracted forms are not used: so the answer, for example, to 'Do elephants have short noses?' is 'They do not', not 'They don't'.

20.1.3 Written enquiries

Focus	Questions with short answers in writing
Age	Any
Level	Elementary–Intermediate
Time	20–30 minutes

Procedure

1 Give each student the name of one other student (see *Teaching tip*, below).

2 Each student takes a piece of paper and writes on it a 'yes/no' question addressed to the person he or she has been allotted. It should be something which he or she is genuinely interested to know, but not anything too personal. For example:

Do you have any brothers and sisters?
Do you like action movies?

3 The paper is then folded, the name of the addressee written on the outside, and the paper passed to the addressee.

4 The addressee writes a short answer. For example:

Yes, I do.
No, I don't.

– but may also add any extra details if he or she wishes. For example:

Yes, I do: one brother.
No, they aren't. I think they're really boring.

5 The note is then returned to the original asker, who asks another, linked question. For example:

Is your brother older than you?
Do you like historical movies?

6 And so the correspondence goes on until everyone has written and answered at least two questions.

7 Invite students who are willing to do so to read some of their exchanges.

Teaching tip

There are various ways of getting students into pairs. The simplest is just to have students working with the person sitting next to them. But if you want to vary, prepare a set of slips with the names of all the students on them, jumble them in a bowl or box, and tell each student to pick one. More elaborate procedures can be based on activities like 8.3 *Find a twin picture* or 7.2.1 *Find someone with the answer*.

20.2 TAG QUESTIONS

20.2.1 It's true, isn't it?

Focus	Tag questions to check or confirm information
Age	Teenager–Adult
Level	Intermediate
Time	15–20 minutes

Procedure

1 Tell the students to write down things that they think they remember about other members of the class or their families or backgrounds, in the form of simple statements. For example:

Anne lived in Argentina for three years.
Don's father is a doctor.

2 Give the class five minutes to write down as many such sentences as they can think of.

3 Tell them to go to the people they have written about and check their information. For example:

Anne, you lived in Argentina for three years, didn't you?
Don, your father is a doctor, isn't he?

4 Students tick the facts they got right and correct the ones they got wrong.

5 Share the various facts in the full class.

Variation

Ask all the students to write up on the board subjects they feel they could answer questions about: special skills, hobbies, jobs, fields of knowledge. Then all the students write down things they think they know about other people's fields of expertise, and check them, as described in *Procedure* above. When answering, the 'experts' may of course add further details and information. At the end, ask students to share new things they have learnt.

Language tip

Tag questions have a falling intonation if the asker is fairly sure of the answer, and a rising one if not. It may be worth demonstrating and perhaps practising this a bit before doing the activities in this section.

20.2.2 Nice day, isn't it?

Focus	Tag questions in casual chat to show expectation of agreement
Age	Teenager–Adult
Level	Intermediate
Time	20–30 minutes
Preparation	Dialogues (see *Box 20.2.2*) copied for students

Procedure

1 Put the students into pairs, and ask each pair to choose one of the dialogues and insert tag questions where they feel the speakers are expecting agreement or sympathy.

2 If they finish, they may add further additions to the dialogue, to make the context clear or to make it funnier or more dramatic.

3 Ask pairs to perform their dialogues as dramatically as possible.

4 After each performance, discuss what is going on.

Box 20.2.2: Nice day, isn't it?

Dialogue 1
A: Nice day.
B: It'll rain tomorrow.
A: Why do you think it'll rain?
B: It's the picnic tomorrow. Always rains for the picnic.
A: You are in a lousy mood today!

Dialogue 2
A: This one looks nice.
B: Oh, yes, a lovely colour. Just matches your eyes.
A: How much is it?
B: Twenty pounds. It's much cheaper than the red one.
A: But the red one will wash better.

Dialogue 3
A: I've really made a mess of things.
B: Well, that's why you're here.
A: I've been such a fool.
B: No, you haven't. We all make mistakes sometimes.
A: It helps, talking to someone about it.

Dialogue 4
A: You know where the microfilm is.
B: I've told you again and again that I don't.
A: We'll just have to help you remember.
B: I can't remember what I don't know.
A: That's what we're going to find out ...

Dialogue 5
A: We are friends?
B: Yes, but ...
A: I wouldn't ask you to do something that was wrong.
B: You haven't told Jean?
A: No, of course not. It'll be a secret between the two of us.

Dialogue 6
A: Very good, Georgie, that's a beautiful picture.
B: I can paint all over Pattie's picture now.
A: No, Georgie, we don't spoil other people's pictures.
B: I do.
A: Now you've made poor little Pattie cry.
B: I don't care.
A: Georgie, that's not the way we talk to our teacher ...

21 Verb structures

21.1 'TO' INFINITIVES

21.1.1 What to do

Focus	'To' infinitive after question words *who*, *where*, *when*, *what*, *whether*, *how*
Age	Teenager–Adult
Level	Intermediate–Advanced
Time	20–30 minutes

Procedure

1 Divide the class into an even number of groups. Half of these groups are told that they are tourists planning to visit this country (wherever this course is taking place). The others are groups of natives of the country.

2 The 'tourists' draw up a list of things they would need to find out. The list begins:

We would need to find out ...

3 Meanwhile the 'natives' draw up a parallel list headed:

We can tell them ...

4 In both cases, the list should consist of phrases like

... where to stay
... where to change money
... what kind of clothes to bring

5 Each 'tourist' group joins up with a native group to ask:

Can you tell us ...?

and are given appropriate information. The native group may also add:

You didn't ask, but we can tell you ...

and may give extra information.

Variation

Tell the 'native' groups that they are the inhabitants of an imaginary island and have to make up the information as they go along. The 'tourists' are thinking of coming to visit their island, so they should make it sound as inviting as possible.

21.1.2 Purposes

Focus	'To' infinitive to express purpose
Age	Any
Level	Elementary–Intermediate
Time	20–25 minutes

Procedure

1 Write on the board a few names of locations: places, local institutions, shops or places of interest (see *Box 21.1.2* for some examples), and elicit suggestions why we might go to each one:

A SUPERMARKET: We'd go there to buy fruit.
THE CAPITAL: We'd go there to see the sights.

2 Erase what you've written, and write up only one location: the bank, for example.

3 Challenge the class to find at least five different purposes for the one you have written up, beginning with 'to ... '. For example:

to get money
to change money
to pay in a cheque
to borrow money
to get a credit card

4 Do the same for two or three other locations.

Follow-up

Divide the class into groups, and ask each group to make its own list of places and write down at least one purpose for each of them. Then groups are invited to read out their purposes, and the rest of the class guess what location they were thinking of.

Box 21.1.2: Purposes

a bank	a post office	a clinic	a disco/nightclub
a school	a hairdresser's	a river	a swimming pool
a beach	a supermarket	a zoo	a petrol/filling station
a park	a restaurant	a gym	a chemist/pharmacist
a theatre	the capital	a pub	a travel agency
a hotel	an airport		

21.1.3 Professional help

Focus	'To' infinitive after verbs like *want* + object
Age	Teenager–Adult
Level	Intermediate–Advanced
Time	30–40 minutes
Preparation	Copy the pictures and headings from the book (see *Boxes 21.1.3b–i*), and paste each onto the top of a separate piece of paper, or download the ready-made worksheets from the CD-ROM.

Procedure

1 Talk about the job of professionals who work with people and need to advise or persuade them. For example, a teacher in a school: what might he/she say to a student (and vice versa)? (Remember they can suggest negative sentences as well as affirmative.) For example:

I want you to do your homework.
I advise you to write down the new words.
I don't expect you to finish your homework today.

And the student might say:

I want you to teach me English.
I'd like the lessons to be interesting.

2 Write on the board a selection of the kinds of verbs that can be used for this activity (see *Box 21.1.3a* for some examples).

3 Put the students into up to eight small groups or pairs, and give each group one of the sheets of paper you have prepared. Tell them to write down on the sheets two or three sentences they can think of that either of the characters in the picture might say or think, using the verbs you have given. They should write **very** clearly.

4 When you see that everyone has written at least two sentences, tell students to pass their sheet to another group, so that everyone has a new one to work on. They add more sentences to the sheets they have received.

5 The groups then pass their sheet to another group which has not seen it yet: and the activity thus continues for three or four more 'rounds'.

6 The sheets are then posted on the classroom wall or left displayed on tables, so that students can go round and see what has been written.

Variations

1 Do stages 1 and 2 of the procedure, relating to fictional characters if you are reading literature with your class, instead of professionals: what does

a particular character in the story want from another? This is a good way into a general discussion of character.

2 Ask teenage students to write down what their parents want, advise, etc. them to do; and comment on them. For example:

> My mother wants me to go to university next year, but I want to take a year off to travel round the world with friends.

Language tip

Note that the verb *suggest* in English works rather differently from other verbs of advising, recommending, etc. You can't say *'I suggest you to do something' as you can say 'I advise you to ...', but have to say 'I suggest doing' or 'I suggest that you ...'. It's worth drawing students' attention to this particular item as it is a common one and the mistake is very widespread with learners from a variety of L1 backgrounds.

Box 21.1.3a: Professional help

Some useful verbs:

advise	force	order	request
allow	get	persuade	teach
ask	help	prefer	tell
encourage	invite	recommend	want
expect	would like	remind	warn

Teaching tip

Having students write out their ideas clearly and then display them, on the wall or on tables, is a nice way of varying the usual 'pooling ideas' oral session at the end of a group-work activity. An alternative is to have them send their work to you in electronic form and then post it on a website.

Box 21.1.3b: Professional help

Box 21.1.3c: Professional help

Box 21.1.3d: Professional help

Box 21.1.3e: Professional help

Box 21.1.3f: Professional help

Box 21.1.3g: Professional help

Vet and dog owner

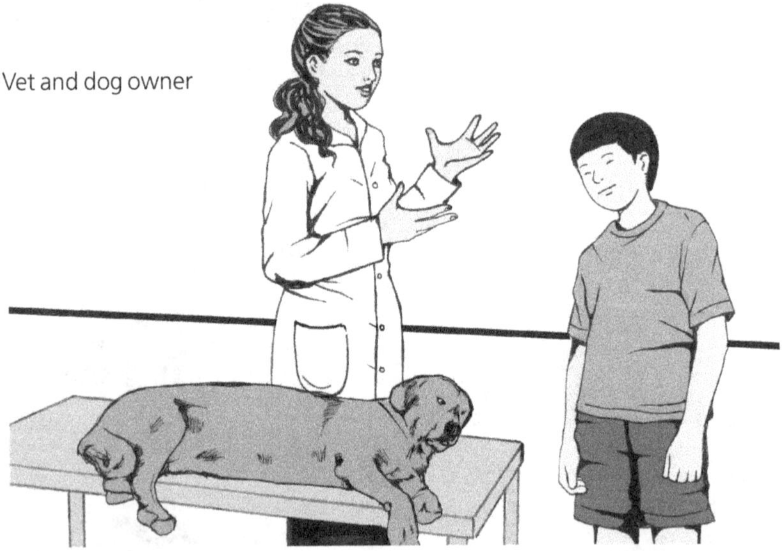

Box 21.1.3h: Professional help

Box 21.1.3i: Professional help

21.2 '-ING' FORMS OF THE VERB

21.2.1 Tastes

Focus	'-ing' forms of the verb after *like, hate, don't mind*
Age	Any
Level	Intermediate
Time	20–25 minutes

Procedure

1 Tell the students to write down on a slip of paper one thing each that they like or love doing, one they hate doing and one they don't mind doing. And do the same yourself. For example:

I love singing; I hate cooking; I don't mind driving.

2 Take in the papers, then read them out one by one, and see if the class can identify each student – and you – by likes and dislikes.

21.2.2 Surveys

Focus	'-ing' forms of the verb after verbs like *enjoy, like, hate,* or as gerunds
Age	Any
Level	Intermediate
Time	30–50 minutes
Preparation	Copies of questionnaires (see *Box 21.2.2a–f*) for students

Procedure

1 The class is divided into groups, each of which gets a different questionnaire; each member of a group has a copy of it.

2 Each member of the group fills in their questionnaire for themselves.

3 The groups then disperse and re-form in such a way that there is at least one representative of each of the original groups in every new group.

4 Participants take turns to ask all other members of the new groups their questions and jot down a tick for each 'yes' or 'no' answer in the appropriate column. They then re-form into the original groupings to pool the answers they have collected and formulate their results into complete sentences, such as:

Most of the class ...
Almost nobody ...

Or, more precisely, if they have time to work out percentages:

30% of our population like driving fast.
10% of our class think smoking is anti-social.

Box 21.2.2a: Surveys

Questionnaire 1	Yes	No
1 Do you think smoking is anti-social?		
2 Do you mind other people smoking near you?		
3 Do you approve of smoking as a habit?		
4 (For smokers) Could you give up smoking easily?		
5 Should the law forbid smoking under the age of 18?		

Box 21.2.2b: Surveys

Questionnaire 2	Yes	No
1 Do you enjoy listening to pop music?		
2 Do you like going to pop music concerts?		
3 Do you mind other people listening to loud pop music near you?		
4 Do you like singing pop songs yourself?		
5 Do you prefer listening on your own?		

Box 21.2.2c: Surveys

Questionnaire 3	Yes	No
1 Do you enjoy eating out?		
2 Do you like eating Italian food?		
3 Could you easily do without eating at restaurants at all?		
4 Do you prefer having your meals at home?		
5 Do you mind paying a lot for a good meal at a restaurant?		

Box 21.2.2d: Surveys

Questionnaire 4	Yes	No
1 Do you enjoy driving?		
2 Do you like driving fast?		
3 Do you dislike other people overtaking you?		
4 Do you ever risk being fined for speeding?		
5 Do you disapprove of people racing each other on the motorway?		

Box 21.2.2e: Surveys

Questionnaire 5	Yes	No
1 Do you enjoy reading books?		
2 Do you enjoy reading newspapers and magazines?		
3 Do you prefer reading to watching television?		
4 Do you like reading before you go to sleep?		
5 Do you sometimes find it difficult to stop reading a good book?		

Box 21.2.2f: Surveys

Questionnaire 6	Yes	No
1 Do you like shopping?		
2 Do you prefer shopping with friends?		
3 Do you enjoy shopping for clothes?		
4 Do you like buying things on the Internet?		
5 Do you prefer shopping in a shopping centre?		

21.2.3 How could you do it?

Focus	Verbs in the '-ing' form after the preposition *by*
Age	Teenager–Adult
Level	Intermediate–Advanced
Time	25–30 minutes
Preparation	Copies of a list of tasks with constraints (see *Box 21.2.3*) for students

Procedure

1 Suggest a simple task. For example:

How do you get someone to come to you?

Then ask for a straightforward solution using *by* + verb + *-ing*:

By calling them.

2 Accept the answer, and then ask if students can think of more ways of achieving this goal, other than just calling. They might suggest:

By making a signal with my hand.

By writing them a note.

3 Give small groups of students a sheet of such tasks, and tell them these are creativity tests: how many different, original ways can they think of to achieve the goals shown?

4 After 10–15 minutes' work, hear their ideas, and decide which group is the winner (the most creative group) for each task.

Follow-up

Students may be asked to design their own tasks, to be exchanged and worked on.

Variation

Make the task more challenging by adding constraints: e.g. how could you get into a (locked) house without a key? How could you pick up a pencil without using your fingers?

Box 21.2.3: How could you do it?

How could you . . .

1 . . . get into a house?

2 . . . pick up a pencil?

3 . . . get someone to look at you?

4 . . . break an egg?

5 . . . move a ball from one side of the room to the other?

6 . . . find out what the time is?

7 . . . persuade someone to do what you want?

8 . . . get someone to laugh?

9 . . . put a baby to sleep?

10 . . . get money?

21.3 VERB OBJECTS

21.3.1 Can I help?

Focus	Direct and indirect objects after ditransitive verbs (verbs with two objects), word order
Age	Any
Level	Intermediate
Time	10–15 minutes
Preparation	Some ideas for situations where you need to do things for other people (see *Box 21.3.1* for some examples)

Procedure

1 Tell the class to imagine they have a friend who needs to learn English – fast. They have unlimited time, money and willingness to help. What might they do?

2 Elicit, or suggest yourself, ideas such as:

I could teach her English myself.
I could buy her a book.
I could recommend a course for her.
I could send her some exercises.

3 Provide some of the other situations, and elicit more ideas, as well as contributing ones yourself.

Note

The 'cues' suggested in *Box 21.3.1* will not necessarily produce sentences with both direct and indirect objects; and some verbs (*suggest, explain*) are tricky in that they don't allow the indirect object pronoun to come before the direct object (e.g. you can't say*'I suggested her the idea' or *'I explained him the problem'). Hence the importance of doing this activity in the full class rather than in groups, so that you can support and if necessary correct their ideas, as well as contributing ones of your own.

Having said that, it is, of course, fine to accept some sentences that don't include direct and indirect objects as well as ones that do, provided that they make sense in the context provided.

Follow-up

Challenge students to think up more situations like this and make appropriate suggestions.

Box 21.3.1: Can I help?

1 Your friend wants to cook a good meal: how can you help him?
2 Your friend isn't happy: how can you cheer her up?
3 Your friend is rather poor: how can you help him get richer?
4 Your little sister can't get to sleep, and your parents are out. What can you do?
5 A friend lives alone, has broken both legs and is in a wheelchair. What can you do to help him?
6 A friend has arrived from a hot country and has no warm clothes. What can you do to help her?
7 An old woman you know is not feeling very well. What can you do for her?

Teaching tip

In an activity with multiple cues, like the one in *21.3.1 Can I help?*, it's a useful teaching strategy to invite students to suggest ideas for any of them, in any order, rather than making them exhaust all ideas for one before moving on to the next, as is conventionally done. But then they have to say: 'For 6' before giving their suggestion: 'I could lend her my old coat'.

21.3.2 Work it out

Focus	Object pronouns with phrasal verbs
Age	Any
Level	Intermediate
Time	25–35 minutes
Preparation	A list of transitive phrasal verbs (see *Box 21.3.2*) shown on the board or copied for students. For homework, tell students to check before the lesson that they know the meanings of all the verbs.

Procedure

1 Distribute copied lists of the phrasal verbs, or display them on the board.

2 Tell the students you are going to give them a hint using one of the verbs and they will have to try to guess what you are thinking of. For example:

  I put them away in the cupboard. (cups)

  or:

  The wind can blow it away. (a piece of paper)

3 Students try to identify what you are thinking of.

4 Invite students to think up similar hints for others to guess and to make up hints similar to yours, based on phrasal verbs. Tell them they may not say simply 'You can ... it ...'. They have to provide some more details, as in the examples above.

5 On their own, students write as many such hints as they can on a piece of paper, using the list of verbs provided. Each such hint should refer to a different object to be guessed.They may work on their own or in pairs.

6 Give the class ten minutes to write their hints, then stop them.

7 Students exchange papers and try to guess and write down what each hint on the paper they have received is referring to. In many cases there may be more than one possible answer: they can write more than one guess for each if they wish.

8 Students get together to check each other's answers.

Follow-up

An interesting advanced vocabulary exercise is to try to find single-word verbs that convey the same meaning as the phrasal verbs.

Variation

Start the activity by brainstorming all the phrasal verbs students can think of, and write these up on the board. Use these as a basis for the activity instead of the ones given here. Such a list will of course include intransitive verbs, like *go away*: so if you do the activity suggested above, not all the hints will involve object pronouns. You might get sentences like: 'It usually goes away if you take an aspirin' (a headache).

Box 21.3.2: Work it out

add up	cut out	let off	show off
ask in	do up	look up	start up
ask out	drink up	make up	switch off
back up	eat up	mix up	switch on
beat up	fill in	pack up	take apart
blow up	fill up	pay back	take away
blow away	get across	pick up	take in
break up	get back	print out	think over
bring about	give away	put away	throw away
bring back	give back	put off	try out
bring out	give out	put on	turn down
bring up	give up	read out	turn off
call up	keep in	ring back	turn on
cheer up	keep out	ring up	use up
clean up	keep up	send back	wear out
close down	leave out	send off	work out
cut off	let down	set up	write down

References and further reading

Academic grammars

Biber, D., Johansson, S., Leech, G., Conrad, S. and Finegan, E. (1999) *Longman Grammar of Spoken and Written English*. Harlow: Pearson Education Limited.

Huddleston, R. and Pullum, G. K. (2002) *The Cambridge Grammar of the English Language*. Cambridge: Cambridge University Press.

Quirk, R., Greenbaum, S., Leech, G. and Svartvik, J. (1985) *A Comprehensive Grammar of the English Language*. London: Longman.

Pedagogical grammar

Swan, M. (2005) *Practical English Usage* (Third Edition). Oxford: Oxford University Press.

Student grammars

Biber, D., Conrad, S. and Leech, G. (2002) *Longman Student Grammar of Spoken and Written English*. Harlow: Pearson Education Limited.

Carter, R. and McCarthy, M. (2006) *Cambridge Grammar of English*. Cambridge: Cambridge University Press.

Grammar-teaching methodology

Celce-Murcia, M. and Larsen-Freeman, D. (1999) *The Grammar Book: An ESL/EFL teacher's course*. Boston: Heinle & Heinle.

Ur, P. (1996) *A Course in Language Teaching*. Cambridge: Cambridge University Press.

Teaching materials and resources

Hancock, M. (1998) *Singing Grammar*. Cambridge: Cambridge University Press.

Nixon, C. and Tomlinson, M. (2003) *Primary Grammar Box*. Cambridge: Cambridge University Press.

Rinvolucri, M. (1986) *Grammar Games*. Cambridge: Cambridge University Press.

Seymour, D. and Popova, M. (2003) *700 Classroom Activities*. London: Macmillan.
Swan, M. and Walter, C. (1997) *How English Works*. Oxford: Oxford University Press.
Swan, M. and Walter, C. (2001) *The Good Grammar Book*. Oxford: Oxford University Press.
Thornbury, S. (2006) *Grammar*. Oxford: Oxford University Press.
Wright, A., Betteridge, D. and Buckby, M. (2006) *Games for Language Learning* (Third Edition). Cambridge: Cambridge University Press.
Zaorob, M. L. and Chin, E. (2001) *Games for Grammar Practice*. Cambridge: Cambridge University Press.

Index

NOTE: Activity titles are shown in **bold**.